Deon Maree

Guitar
TEACH YOURSELF

TAFELBERG

Dedicated to my friends Piet and Paul

© 1991 Tafelberg Publishers Ltd,
28 Wale Street, Cape Town

Photographs by Bernard Clark
Typography and design by Wim Reinders & Associates, Cape Town
Cover design by Abdul Amien
Set in 10/12 pt Plantin by National Book Printers, Goodwood, Cape
Printed and bound by National Book Printers, Goodwood, Cape

First edition 1991
First impression 1991

ISBN 0 624 03013 X

CONTENTS

PREFACE

I was fourteen years old and away at a weekend camp when I first became interested in the guitar. That Saturday night we had a camp-fire concert and one of the boys played and sang two songs from the movie *Katrina*. I was enthralled. That very same evening, I vowed that I was also going to learn to play the guitar.

I learnt my first couple of chords on a guitar I borrowed from a friend at the hostel where I was staying.

Then, when I was sixteen, I contracted jaundice and had to spend four weeks in bed. One day, my brother unexpectedly came into my room, carrying a guitar. My family had decided to club together to buy me a guitar as a surprise. Day after day I sat cross-legged on my bed and played over and over again the few chords I knew. By the end of the fourth week, I could play *House of the Rising Sun* exactly as it sounded on the record.

While learning to play, I went through what seemed like endless frustration. I battled for hours on end, spent days with sore fingertips and had very real doubts as to whether I would ever be able to play properly. But every new song I learnt rekindled my enthusiasm. And although I struggled in the beginning, I realise now it was definitely worth the effort, when I think of all the friends I have made through playing the guitar, the great sense of satisfaction I feel on finally mastering a new piece of music and, above all, the pleasure it gives me to be able to play for other people.

The seven chapters in this book cover the fundamental aspects of the art of playing the guitar. The book is set out as systematically and simply as possible so that anyone with a little patience and perseverance, and enough enthusiasm, will be able to learn to play this marvellous instrument.

DEON MAREE
March 1991

1 GUITARS

Kinds of guitar

Acquiring your first guitar may not be as simple as it sounds.

To the novice, the wide range of guitars available in the shops can be quite confusing. We will, therefore, start by discussing the different kinds of guitar and their particular uses.

CLASSICAL GUITAR

The classical guitar, also known as the nylon-string or Spanish guitar, is the oldest kind of guitar. Its shape and design have changed little over the past 150 years.

The strings of the classical guitar are made of nylon – the three thin strings are simply nylon strands, while each of the three bass strings is a nylon core encased by thin copper wire.

Because this is the easiest guitar on which to learn to play, it is particularly popular with beginners.

The classical guitar has a tender, warm, sensitive sound.

head

machine head

capstan

neck

sound-box

sound-hole

nut

bridge

first string

saddle

sixth string

fret

ACOUSTIC STEEL-STRING GUITAR

At the beginning of this century, the acoustic steel-string guitar was developed from the classical guitar as an instrument to accompany singing.

It is a very versatile instrument and is used by vocal groups, bands and especially by folk-singers.

The steel-string guitar has a strong, clear and vibrant sound.

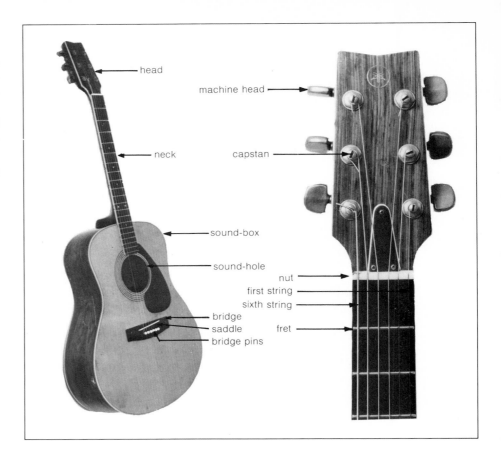

head
machine head
neck
capstan
sound-box
sound-hole
nut
first string
sixth string
bridge
saddle
fret
bridge pins

ELECTRIC GUITAR

The electric guitar is a product of the electronic age. It is an extremely popular instrument in rock 'n' roll and pop music.

Because it is played through an amplifier, the electric guitar can be played at very high volume. There is a vast assortment of electronic accessories which one can use to change the sound. This means that an almost unlimited variety of sounds is possible.

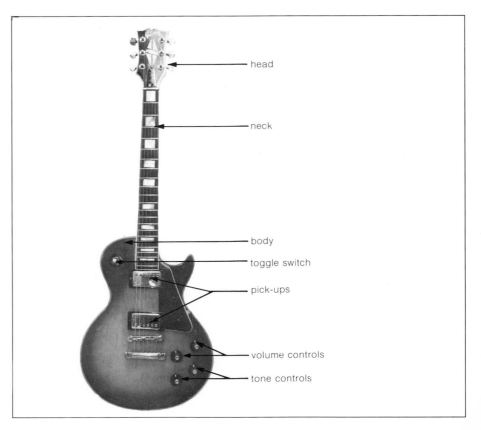

head
neck
body
toggle switch
pick-ups
volume controls
tone controls

Hollow-body electric guitar

Because the body of this electric guitar is hollow like that of the acoustic guitar, and because it has two pick-ups like the conventional electric guitar, you might easily be mistaken into thinking that a hollow-body electric guitar is a combination of an acoustic *and* an electric guitar.

Most hollow-body guitars don't have much of an acoustic sound, however, and they also don't have the specific characteristics of a solid-body guitar. The hollow-body electric guitar has a very distinctive sound that makes it particularly popular with jazz guitarists.

Bass guitar

Many of the basic techniques and principles involved in playing a conventional guitar also apply to the bass guitar.

The four strings of the bass guitar are tuned the same way as the four bass strings of an ordinary guitar, except they are an octave lower. If you know the notes on the guitar, you will actually know them on the bass guitar too.

Many bass guitarists learn to play on a normal six-string guitar first, and only later make the fairly easy transition to the bass guitar.

Twelve-string guitar

The twelve-string guitar looks exactly like the normal steel-string guitar except that it has six pairs of strings instead of six single strings.

Once you can play a normal guitar, it is very easy to adapt to the twelve-string. The beginner might, however, find that he has trouble tuning all twelve strings.

The twelve-string guitar has a full, ringing sound and is a good accompaniment for solo vocalists and vocal groups.

Choosing a guitar

Before buying a guitar, you must, therefore, first decide which of the three basic kinds of guitar you are interested in: the classical, the steel-string acoustic or the electric guitar.

These three different kinds of guitar all have certain advantages, but they are not equally suitable for a beginner to learn on.

☐ The owner of an **electric guitar** gives the following advice: "My Gibson? I'd sell my car, I'd sell my clothes, but never my Gibson. Where would I ever get another guitar like that?

"I still have my old acoustic guitar at home, but I can't play it in the band. When we recorded our LP, I did play my acoustic guitar on some of the tracks, but that was in the studio where you can hear the guitar well. On stage, I really need my Gibson. It can scream, it can be gentle, it can give a really punchy beat.

"But you actually want to know whether *you* should buy a guitar like that. If you have the money, go ahead. But any electric guitar easily costs a couple of hundred rand, and then you still have to buy an amplifier on top of that. Few people have that kind of money.

"Be patient. Get yourself a nice acoustic guitar. When you can play well enough to think about joining a band, *then* you can consider buying yourself a new, expensive electric guitar."

☐ The owner of an **acoustic guitar** states his point of view: "So, you want to buy a guitar? Have you heard mine? What a guitar!

"You can't really expect to buy a guitar like this when you buy your first guitar. Most people first learn to play on some beaten-up old thing.

"It took me so long to save up enough for my first guitar, that I learnt quite a number of songs on a friend's guitar while I was saving to buy my own.

"Eventually, I was so impatient to have my own guitar that I bought the cheapest one I could find – a real bicycle shop special. It looked so beautiful in the shop window, hanging between the bicycle wheels, fishing rods and paraffin lamps!

"Unfortunately, it wasn't possible to play it. The strings cut right through my fingertips. And no matter how hard I tried, I just couldn't tune it. I started to think that my musical ear was so bad that I would never make a musician. When my friend tried to tune the guitar, he just said, 'Nobody can tune this piece of junk.' So I borrowed his guitar again, though his patience was wearing thin.

"Eventually, I got a loan from my father and bought myself this acoustic steel-string guitar. I'm *extremely* happy with it – it sounds better and better every year.

"If you have the money, buy yourself a good steel-string guitar. You won't be sorry."

☐ Finally, let us turn to the owner of a **classical guitar**: "Can you play chords yet? Not yet? Then the classical guitar is just the guitar for you. It is definitely the easiest guitar to learn to play on. Because the strings are made of nylon, they are soft and give way easily, which makes it a lot easier to finger chords. Your fingers won't hurt nearly as much.

"The strings are also slightly further apart than those on a steel-string guitar, which makes it a lot easier for inexperienced fingers to form the chords correctly.

"Then there is also the matter of tuning. I've seen quite a number of steel-string guitars that are quite impossible to tune, but I've seldom seen a nylon-string guitar that can't be tuned perfectly. This is because nylon strings are subject to far less tension. Manufacturers can, therefore, produce cheap nylon-string guitars without having to worry about the neck warping under the strain of the strings.

"Yes, if I were the one who wanted to learn to play, I would go for a nylon-string guitar."

No matter who says what, remember that *you* are the one who will be playing on your guitar. Each of the three kinds of guitar has specific features. You may be interested in some of these features, especially if you have already progressed beyond the first few basic chords on a borrowed guitar.

Within the range of what you can afford, buy the guitar that *you* would most like to play.

Buying a guitar

If you know someone who can play the guitar, ask him or her to go with you when you go shopping for a guitar, especially when it comes to making your final choice. It will help a great deal if you can rely on the judgement of someone who knows the instrument well.

You could also look in the newspapers for a good second-hand guitar, or ask around among friends and family. Buying second-hand can be a bit of a risk, but your chances of getting a bargain are better.

A golden rule when buying any expensive item is to shop around as much as possible before you decide. Get an overall picture of what is available and at what price. Concentrate on shops that stock a large selection. Ask the salesman if you can take the guitars down from their stands. Then listen to the sound of each guitar. This way, you will get an idea of the quality available in each price range.

When judging a guitar, consider the following points:

☐ *Tuning:* Ask the salesman to tune the guitar with an electronic tuner. Make sure that the guitar stays in tune in all the different chords. If there is something wrong with the construction of a guitar, the tuning will be the most obviously affected. So make absolutely sure that the guitar is not in tune in one chord, but out of tune in another. The three chords where this will be the most obvious are E, G and D.

☐ *Action:* The action of a guitar determines the ease with which a chord can be fingered. This depends to a large degree on how far the strings are from the frets. If there is something wrong with the action, you will find it difficult to finger the chords properly.

☐ *Scratch or bump marks:* Even the most minute little scratch reduces the value of a guitar. You should, therefore, insist on a discount if the instrument is shop-soiled.

□ *Sound:* Even if you cannot play the guitar at all, you can still decide which guitar sounds best to you. Remember that the loudest guitar is not necessarily the best. A good guitar has a sensitive, warm, full sound.

□ *Feel:* Hold every guitar you consider buying, even if you do not really know how to play. Finger a few chords and strum over the strings. The guitar that "talks" to you, that feels right, is probably the right choice.

□ *Guitar case:* Ensure that the price of the guitar includes a guitar case or bag. If not, add it to the price of the guitar.

□ *Strings:* A good guitar is sometimes fitted with such old strings that you cannot judge its real value. If you are seriously considering buying the guitar, ask the salesman to fit a new set of strings. If you are buying a steel-string guitar, you may find that the strings are of such a heavy gauge that they hurt your fingers when you hold down a chord. Ask the salesman to fit a new set of a lighter gauge, even if you have to pay a little extra; he might even give you the strings free of charge.

When you have finally chosen and bought a guitar, ask the salesman to tune it accurately with an electronic tuner. You should also buy a tuning fork in E (see page 16) or a set of pitch-pipes.

Never be in a hurry to decide on a guitar. Just make sure that the guitar you choose is the right one for you.

Taking care of your guitar

The owner of a new guitar is usually so protective of his acquisition that advice on caring for it is almost superfluous. Nevertheless, here are a few hints:

When you fit a new set of strings to your guitar, this is a good time to polish it as well, especially on the fretboard. You should be able to find guitar polish at any good music shop. You can also use violin polish, which in my opinion works even better.

Always wipe the strings with a cloth when you have finished playing. This removes moisture and dirt from the strings and ensures that they will sound clear for much longer.

Take care that no-one knocks your guitar over or – awful thought – steps on it. Always put your guitar in a safe place or keep it in its case when you are not playing.

When you have to leave your guitar in a car, put it in the boot where no-one can see it. If there is no room in the boot, cover it with clothes or a newspaper.

Avoid subjecting your guitar to sudden changes in temperature or humidity, and always keep it away from heaters and direct sunlight.

Strings

New strings need a couple of days to stretch completely and to stabilise. Many guitarists have experienced the frustration of fitting a new set of strings for a special occasion, only to discover that their guitar simply will not stay in tune.

To make the strings stabilise more quickly, try pulling them away from the body, one string at a time. But be careful not to overdo it and damage the strings in the process.

Never tune guitar strings higher than standard pitch (see page 15), since both the guitar and strings are manufactured to give the best results at standard pitch. If you tune the strings too high (too taut), you will put too much strain on the neck of the guitar, which can damage it.

Be careful not to make a nip or bend in a string when you take it out of the packet or when you fit it. A nip in a string will spoil its sound and can cause it to break easily.

If one of the strings keeps breaking at the same place, check that the string is not being damaged by a sharp point. If there is a sharp edge, smooth it down by sandpapering it.

Never put steel strings on a nylon-string guitar. Steel strings need to be at too high a tension for the construction of a nylon-string guitar and will damage the guitar. Although nylon strings can be fitted to a steel-string guitar without damaging it, this is not worth the effort because the guitar will produce a very poor sound.

If you are uncertain whether a guitar was originally intended to have steel or nylon strings, compare it with photos of classical and steel-string guitars. Take particular note of the head and bridge of the guitar.

Replacing strings

CLASSICAL GUITAR

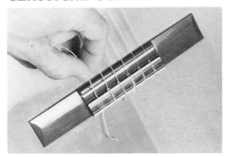

One end of the string is soft. Thread this end through the hole in the bridge.

Pull the end back over the bridge and thread it through underneath the string.

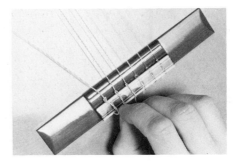

Wind the end around the string two or three times and then pull the string taut. The end that is left must be short enough not to rattle against the sound-box.

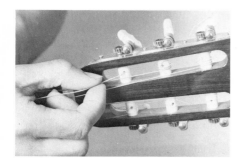

Turn the machine head until the hole through the capstan is facing upwards. Thread the end of the string through the hole from above.

Wind the end around the capstan and then thread it through underneath the string.

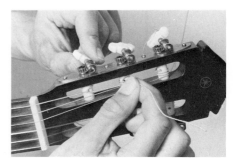

Pull the end of the string taut while turning the machine head.

STEEL-STRING GUITAR

Ensure that the string is slack before trying to remove the bridge pin. If you have trouble removing it, hook either a coin or a teaspoon under the pin and use the one next to it as a pivot to jiggle it loose.

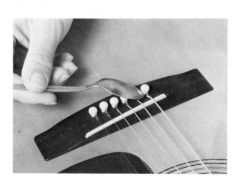

When fitting a new string, make sure that when you push the bridge pin into the hole to fasten the string, the ball at the end of the string does not get stuck under the pin, since the pin will then be pulled out when you tighten the string.

Wind the string around the capstan a few times.

Thread the string through the hole and pull it away from the fretboard while turning the machine head.

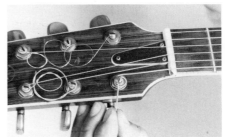

2 TUNING

Starting to tune

It is quite normal to be unable to tune your guitar perfectly the first few times. Don't think that your musical ear is letting you down. You are, in fact, expecting your ear to perform a very new and rather strange task. Your ear actually has to be taught to distinguish between a slightly lower note and a slightly higher one.

Give your ear plenty of practice. Always tune your guitar before you start playing, even if your efforts are not always very successful.

There is more than one way to tune a guitar, and each person eventually develops his own method. Experiment with the different methods until you find one or a combination of methods which enables you to tune your guitar perfectly.

Each string has its own machine head, which you must turn in order to tune the string.

When you turn the machine head in one direction, the string becomes slack and the note becomes lower. In the opposite direction the string gets tighter and the note higher.

NOTES OF THE STRINGS

Standard pitch

Guitars and guitar strings are manufactured in such a way as to produce the best results when the strings are tuned to standard pitch. If the strings are tuned too high, you will find it harder to finger the chords. It could also damage your guitar and you might find that the strings break more easily. If the strings are tuned too low, this will spoil the sound and cause the strings to buzz against the frets.

You will need another instrument in order to tune your guitar to standard pitch. Tuning forks, pitch-pipes and electronic tuners are specifically made for this purpose. You can also tune to standard pitch using another guitar, a piano, an electronic keyboard, a harmonica, a recorder or some other wind instrument.

It is necessary to tune only one string to standard pitch. You can then tune the rest of the strings according to that string.

PITCH-PIPES

A pitch-pipe is a small instrument with six whistles that give the notes of the six strings. Apart from being small and inexpensive, it is also easy to use – you simply blow through each whistle in turn and tune each string according to the note played.

Some people find it difficult at first to tune a guitar using pitch-pipes, because the sound of the whistle differs from that of the plucked string. The secret is not to listen to the sound of the note, but to the pitch. It is important to blow softly and evenly through the whistles. If you blow too hard, you will force the note out of tune.

TUNING FORK

A tuning fork is the most reliable instrument for determining standard pitch. It is small enough to keep handy at all times and, after ten years, will be just as accurate as on the day you bought it.

A, C and E tuning forks are available. If you have a choice, buy an E tuning fork, since with an A or C tuning fork you will have to finger a note on the guitar, which can complicate matters. The E tuning fork, on the other hand, is made especially for the guitar and gives the E note of the unfingered first string.

Use the tuning fork as follows:
☐ Hold the stem between your thumb and index finger, and tap the prongs against your knee.
☐ Press the end against the body of the guitar (see photo) to make the note sound loud and clear.
☐ Pluck the unfingered first (thinnest) string with your left hand.

PIANO, ORGAN OR KEYBOARD

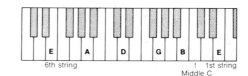

You can play the notes of the six strings of the guitar on a piano, organ or keyboard, as shown on the diagram.

When tuning from a piano, press the right-hand pedal down to make the note last longer.

When tuning from an organ or electronic keyboard, choose an "instrument" with a long and even note, such as the flute. Switch off any effect such as vibrato to get a clear note from which to tune.

ELECTRONIC TUNER

If after weeks of trying, you still can't manage to tune your guitar and your patience has run out, you should consider buying yourself an electronic tuner.

It is extremely easy to tune with this gadget. Simply pluck one string at a time, turning the machine head until the needle of the tuner shows that the string is in tune.

An electronic tuner is especially useful when two guitarists who still have difficulty in tuning their guitars want to play together. It is also a very useful instrument to have in a band.

However, this electronic marvel costs nearly as much as a cheap guitar. So you will have to consider the costs carefully before buying one.

Relative tuning

There are a number of methods in which to tune the rest of the strings according to the string tuned to standard pitch.

The best-known and most popular method is relative tuning. Relative tuning works on the basis that if you depress the second string at a specific place on the fretboard, you will get the note of the unfingered first string. In this way, the second string is tuned according to the first string, the third string according to the second string, the fourth according to the third, and so on until all the strings are tuned.

The disadvantage of relative tuning is that if you make a mistake along the way, the rest of the strings will all be out of tune. For this reason, it is advisable when using relative tuning, to double-check the tuning using another method.

RELATIVE TUNING

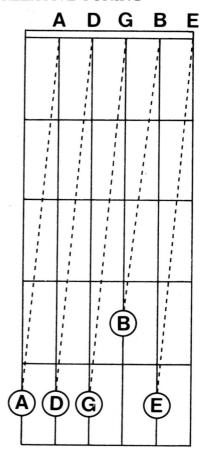

Depress the **second string** behind the fifth fret. This is the same note (E) as that of the unfingered first string.

Pluck the two strings in quick succession. If the two notes sound as if they do not have the same pitch, turn the machine head of the second string until they sound the same. Pluck the string before turning the machine head so that you can hear if the note is getting higher or lower.

When the second string is in tune, the **third string** is tuned according to the same method, except that in this case, the string should be depressed behind the fourth fret, and not the fifth – the only exception.

Next, depress the **fourth string** behind the fifth fret. The note should correspond with the open (unfingered) third string.

Depress the **fifth string** behind the fret and tune according to the open fourth string.

Finally, depress the **sixth string** behind the fifth fret and tune according to the open fifth string.

Tuning tips

☐ Always tune *from low to high*. If you are not sure whether a string is too low or too high, always tune it down first. Then, as you tune the string higher, you will find it easier to hear when the string is in tune. This also reduces the risk of breaking the string by tuning it too high. In addition, a string stays in tune better if it is tuned from low to high (turned tighter).

☐ Pluck the strings *in quick succession*, not simultaneously. This makes it easier to distinguish between them.

☐ Pluck the string *while you are turning the machine head* so that you can hear the note getting higher or lower.

☐ To tune finely, listen to the *waves* of the sound the strings make. When the two strings are nearly in tune, you will hear uneven, tremulous waves. But when the strings are perfectly in tune, it will sound as if the two notes form one smooth, even wave. Experiment with this – it is the secret to accurate tuning.

☐ To make the note ring out long and clear, play the string using a *rest stroke*. In other words, the finger or plectrum that plucks the string rests on the next string at the end of the movement (see page 54).

Tuning according to E notes

One of the most effective ways of double-checking a relative tuning is to compare the E note on all six strings.

Knowing where E can be found on each string is also a good starting point from which to learn the rest of the notes on the fretboard.

The E note on each string:

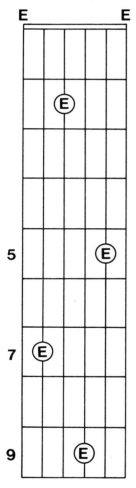

Experiment by comparing different strings with each other, for instance the open first string with the open sixth string, or the open sixth string with the fifth string fingered behind the seventh fret, and so on.

This is also an easy way to determine which string is out of tune when you can hear a note is false, but are not sure exactly where the fault lies.

Tuning with harmonics

Learning to play harmonics takes a bit of practice, but this is a very popular and probably one of the most effective ways to tune a guitar.

A harmonic produces a long, even note that gives you enough time to tune the string before the note fades away.

As explained earlier, two notes that are not perfectly in tune produce an uneven, tremulous wave. This undulating wave is especially noticeable when tuning with harmonics. You hardly have to listen to the pitch of the notes; you need really concentrate only on the waves themselves.

Harmonics are played by touching a string lightly and then removing your finger the moment the string is played. The string should not be pressed right down to touch the fret. In fact, your finger should rest only lightly on the string.

The string is not touched *behind* the fret, as when a note is fingered, but directly *above* the fret.

There are only a few places on the strings where harmonics can be played – they sound clearest when played above the fifth, seventh and twelfth frets.

To make the note last longer, it can be played using a rest stroke.

TUNING WITH HARMONICS

Compare the sixth string's fifth fret harmonic with the open first string.

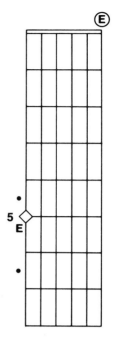

Compare the sixth string's seventh fret harmonic with the open second string.

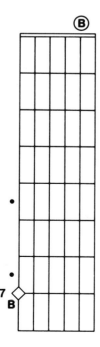

18

Compare the sixth string's fifth fret harmonic with the fifth string's seventh fret harmonic.

Compare the fifth string's fifth fret harmonic with the fourth string's seventh fret harmonic.

Compare the fourth string's fifth fret harmonic with the third string's seventh fret harmonic.

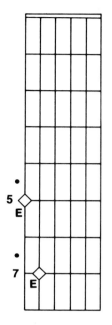

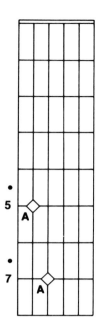

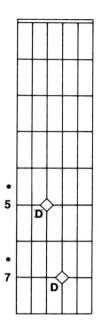

Tuning according to a central string

The big advantage of this method is that all the strings are tuned according to one specific string. This means that if another string is not perfectly tuned, at least it will not influence the tuning of the rest of the strings.

This is also an effective way to double-check the accuracy of relative tuning.

FIRST STRING
AS CENTRAL
STRING

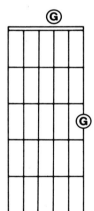

Tune the open fifth string according to the first string depressed behind the fifth fret.

Tune the open third string according to the first string depressed behind the third fret.

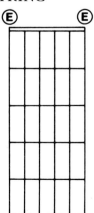

Tune the open sixth string according to the open first string.

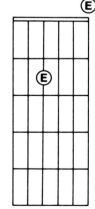

Tune the fourth string depressed behind the second fret according to the open first string.

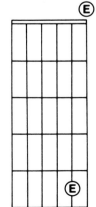

Tune the second string depressed behind the fifth fret according to the open first string.

19

FOURTH STRING AS CENTRAL STRING

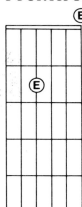 Tune the open first string according to the fourth string depressed behind the second fret.

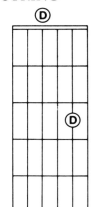 Tune the second string depressed behind the third fret according to the open fourth string.

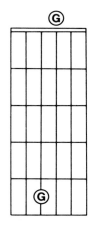 Tune the open third string according to the fourth string depressed behind the fifth fret.

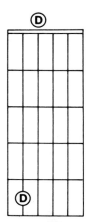 Tune the fifth string depressed behind the fifth fret according to the open fourth string.

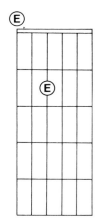 Tune the open sixth string according to the fourth string depressed behind the second fret.

3 CHORDS

Starting to play

If you strum across the strings of your guitar without depressing any of the strings with your left hand, you will hear that something sounds wrong. This is because the notes of these unfingered strings do not form a musical unit. Some of the strings must be depressed for the notes to form a harmonious whole.

To be able to play the guitar, you must start by learning to press the strings in certain combinations so that they sound well together – in other words, you must learn to finger chords. Fortunately, fingering chords is quite simple.

CHORD DIAGRAMS

The standard method of writing down chords is in the form of chord diagrams. A chord diagram represents the neck of the guitar.

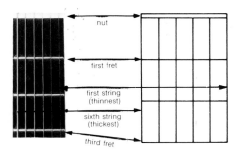

The diagram shows which finger should depress which string. For this purpose, the fingers of the left hand have been numbered (excluding the thumb, which is seldom used to depress the strings).

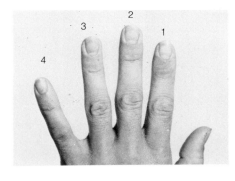

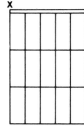

In some chords, certain strings don't form part of the chord. Where this is the case, the string is not played and is marked with an X on the chord diagram.

X = Do not play the string

Left-handed players

It is only natural to be stronger on one side of the body than on the other. If you are left-handed, you should play the rhythm with your left hand.

This means that the strings of your guitar must be turned around so that the bass strings are still at the top. Remember to turn the nut around as well; the width of the grooves in the nut varies according to the thickness of the strings. Bear in mind, too, that guitars made specifically for left-handed players are also available.

A left-handed player may find that the chord diagrams sometimes seem upside down. The best solution to this problem is to practise in front of a mirror.

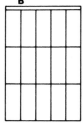

The root of a chord is the note on which the chord is built. Each chord's bass root is important for strumming and fingerpicking and is discussed in the next chapter.

B = Bass root

Learning to finger chords

Finger the E chord as shown.

Strum across the strings with the thumb or index finger of your right hand. Play each string in turn to be sure they all sound clear.

You may have to exert considerable pressure to get a clear sound from the fingered strings, as your fingertips are still soft and not very strong. Although you may feel that your fingers will never be strong enough to depress the strings properly, as your fingertips harden and your fingers get used to this new action, you will gradually find you need less force to make a fingered string sound clear.

A good exercise when learning to finger a chord is to lift your fingers slightly – about 5 mm – from the strings. Then finger the chord again and strum across the strings. Lift your fingers from the strings again, then press down and strum.

In the beginning, your fingers will tend to get mixed up when you lift them from the strings, but the more you repeat the exercise, the more easily your fingers will hold the pattern.

This is the secret of learning to finger chords: your fingers have to learn to form certain patterns. If you repeat a pattern often enough, you will find that your fingers form the pattern by themselves. And once your fingers have learnt one pattern, it becomes easier to learn the next one.

TIPS ON FINGERING CHORDS

☐ Press your thumb against the back of the guitar neck. Without the help of your thumb, fingering chords will be a pulling action, whereas if you use your thumb, this becomes a proper pressing action, with more force for less work.

☐ Make sure that the neck of the guitar does not rest in the palm of your hand – this will hinder the movement and positioning of your fingers.

☐ Make sure that you depress each string right behind the fret. Although

E CHORD

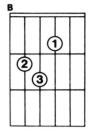

The E chord is fingered as follows:

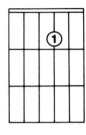

Depress the third string behind the first fret with your first finger (the index finger of your left hand).

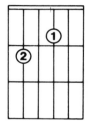

While keeping your first finger in place, depress the fifth string behind the second fret with your second finger.

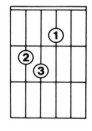

Then depress the fourth string behind the second fret with your third finger.

you cannot depress the fifth string of the E chord right behind the fret (the third finger is in the way), try to keep your finger as close to the fret as possible. The closer it is, the less force you will need to make the string sound clear.

☐ Are any of your fingers touching the string below the one they should be depressing? If you touch a string without depressing it properly, it cannot vibrate and thus cannot sound.

NAILS
To depress the strings easily, the nails of the left hand need to be short.

Long nails press against the fretboard behind the strings and prevent your fingertip from depressing the string properly. To compensate, you then have to tilt your finger, which reduces the amount of pressure you exert on the string. Also when you tilt your finger, it may touch the next string, which will prevent it from sounding or cause it to buzz. To check whether your nails are the right length, press each finger down perpendicular to a flat surface: your nail should not touch the surface.

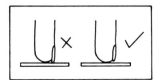

WAYS TO HOLD THE GUITAR
For the beginner, the best way to hold the guitar is definitely the method used by classical guitarists.

Sit forward on your chair with your legs apart and with the guitar resting between your legs. The left leg should be slightly higher than the right leg. One way of doing this is to place your left foot on a pile of books. Classical guitarists normally use a foot rest, but this is not really worth buying if you are not going to specialise in classical guitar.

In this position, your guitar should not move when you take your hands away from it. This is the big advantage of the classical position – it gives your hands complete freedom of movement.

You have probably seen guitarists playing in all kinds of strange positions. Later, when you are quite familiar with the guitar, you will be able to hold it in just about any position you can imagine. However, while you are still learning, it is better to hold the guitar in one of the more conventional positions.

Classical position

Firstly, check that your guitar is not leaning forwards or backwards. This will force your hands into an uncomfortable position, making it harder for you to finger chords and

hindering the movement of your right hand. Do not tip the guitar back in order to see your left hand; rather lean slightly forward *over* the guitar.

An alternative to the classical position, and one which is used by women in particular, is to cross your legs and let the curve of the guitar rest on your thigh.

When you are familiar with the classical position, you can put away the pile of books and use your left foot as a foot rest.

Learning to change chords

As soon as you are able to finger the A chord, you can start changing between the A and the E chord. Finger the A chord and strum across the strings, then change to the E chord, strumming across the strings again. Then return to the A chord.

With time, your fingers will learn the quickest route from the chord they are holding to the next chord to be played. All you have to do is let them follow the route over and over again, until they eventually know this route instinctively.

Although you might feel that you are only learning to change between two chords, you are actually learning the process of chord changing itself.

Learning to finger chords and to change between them is really a physical exercise. You could even describe these movements as push-ups or fitness exercises for your fingers.

Even though you may not be aware that your chord-changing techniques are improving daily, they will get better with each exercise. As with all physical exercise, repetition is what really works. Change, press, strum; change, press, strum . . .

Basic chords

B = bass root
X = do not play the string
m = minor
7 = seventh

A CHORD

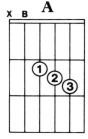 

The A chord is fingered as follows:

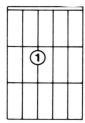 

Depress the fourth string behind the second fret with your first finger.

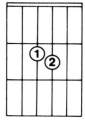 

Depress the third string behind the second fret with your second finger.

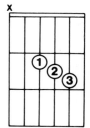 

Depress the second string behind the second fret with your third finger.

Remember not to play the sixth string. It is not part of the chord.

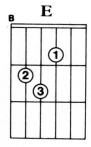 

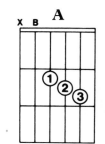 

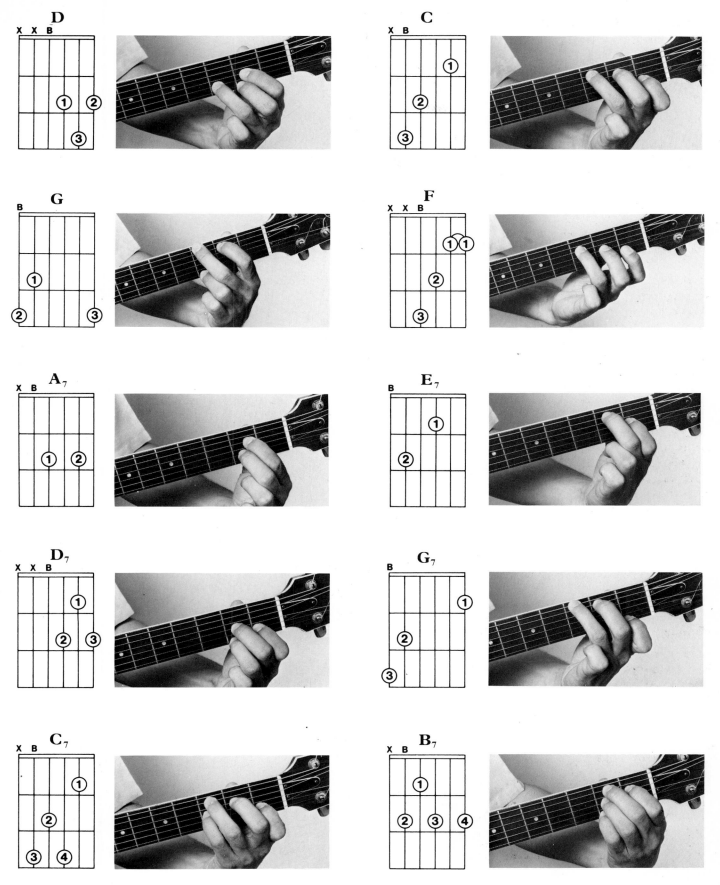

25

Em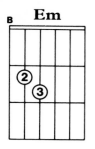

Am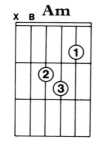

Dm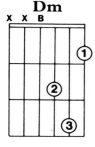

Bm

B = bass root
X = do not play the string
m = minor
7 = seventh

Starting to sing along

As soon as you can play the three main chords of a key, you can quite easily learn to accompany yourself on the guitar.

Learning to play songs is a quick and easy way to derive pleasure from your guitar playing. It is also good practice in fingering and chord changing.

The simplest way to learn to accompany singing on the guitar is to strum once across the strings at the start of each measure.

If you look at the songs on the following pages, you will see that the measures are indicated by slashes. At every slash, you should strum once across the strings, while fingering the right chord.

By keeping the movement of your right hand as simple as possible in the beginning, you will be able to concentrate on your singing and the finger-ing of the chords. It is important to be sure of the melody of the song you want to learn to play. When someone sings out of tune, it is usually because he or she is not sure *which* notes to sing.

Before singing with the guitar, sing the song a few times without accompaniment so as to refresh your memory. It also helps a lot if you sing the song over and over again for a couple of days until you have memorised the tune. The more familiar you are with the lyrics and the tune, the easier it will be to learn to play the song on the guitar.

If you do not wish to sing, then you can whistle the melody. It is actually a good idea to whistle a lot anyway, because this makes you more familiar with the melody and helps develop your musical ear. Often you can also hear a tune better when you whistle rather than sing it. So if you're not too

sure of a tune, try to whistle it first. Your ear will be able to hear the notes more clearly and you will stand a better chance of singing the melody correctly.

Before you start to sing with the guitar, first strum the song's chords a few times. If the song is, for example, in the key of A, play the chords A, D, E and A so that your ear can identify the key, just as the organist in a church always plays a few chords at the beginning of each hymn.

To summarise, learn each song in the following three stages:

1. Sing the song a few times without accompaniment to be sure of the melody.
2. Play the main chords of the song so that your ear can identify the key.
3. Then sing the song, strumming once across the strings at the start of each measure.

26

Songs for practice

Key of A

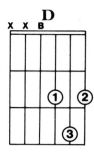
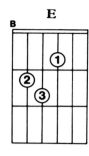

MICHAEL, ROW THE BOAT ASHORE 4/4
Traditional

_____

      A
Michael, /row the boat a-/shore,

     D A
Halle-/lu-/jah;

               E
Michael, /row the boat a-/shore,

     A E A
Halle-/lu-/u-/jah.

Sister help to trim the sails,
Hallelujah;
Sister help to trim the sails,
Hallelujah.

Jordan's river is chilly and cold,
Hallelujah;
Chills the body but warms the soul,
Hallelujah.

Jordan's river is deep and wide,
Hallelujah;
Meet my mother on the other side,
Hallelujah.

KUMBAYA 2/4
Traditional

_____

  A   D   A
/Kumba-/ya, my /Lord, | /kumba-/ya, | |

                          D   E
/Kumba-/ya, my /Lord, | /kumba-/ya, | |

         A   D   A
/Kumba-/ya, my /Lord, | /kumba-/ya, | |

D   A   E   A
/Oh, /Lord, /kumba-/ya. | |

Someone's singing, my Lord, kumbaya   (3X)
Someone's dancing, my Lord, kumbaya   (3X)
Someone's weeping, my Lord, kumbaya   (3X)
Someone's shouting, my Lord, kumbaya   (3X)
Someone's praying, my Lord, kumbaya   (3X)
Kumbaya, my Lord, kumbaya (3X).

HE'S GOT THE WHOLE WORLD IN HIS HANDS 4/4
Traditional

_____

             A
He's got the /whole world /in His hands,

            E₇
He's got the /whole world /in His hands,

            A
He's got the /whole world /in His hands,

           E₇   A
He's got the /whole world in His /hands.

He's got the wind and the rain in His hands,
He's got the sun and the moon in His hands,
He's got the wind and the rain in His hands,
He's got the whole world in His hands.

He's got you and me, brother, in His hands, etc.

He's got the little bitty baby, in His hands, etc.

He's got everybody in His hands, etc.

Key of D

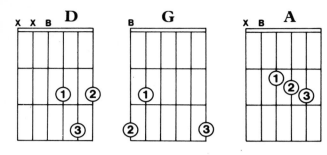

RED RIVER VALLEY 4/4
Traditional

           D   A₇   D
From this /valley they /say you are /going, /

                                         A₇
We will /miss your bright /eyes and sweet /smile; /

          D   D₇   G   Em
For they /say you are /taking the /sunshine /

          D   A₇   D
That has /brightened our /pathways a-while. /

             D   A₇   D
Come and /sit by my /side, if you /love me, /

                    A₇
Do not /hasten to /bid me a-/dieu,

          D   D₇   G   Em
Just re-/member the /Red river /valley /

          D   A₇   D
And the /cowboy who /loved you so /true. /

I've been thinking a long time my darling,
Of the sweet words you never would say,
Now, alas, must my fond hopes all vanish?
For they say you are going away.
(Chorus)

Do you think of this valley you're leaving?
Oh, how lonely, how sad it will be.
Do you think of the kind hearts you're breaking?
And the grief you are causing to me?
(Chorus)

They will bury me where you have wandered,
Near the hills where the daffodils grow,
When you're gone from the Red river valley,
For I can't live without you I know.
(Chorus)

SLOOP JOHN B 4/4
Traditional

          D
We /sailed on the sloop John /B

My /grandaddy and /me,

                         A
/Round the seven /seas we did /roam. /

                 D   G
Drinking all /night, /we got into a /fight, /

   D   A   D
I /feel so lonesome, /I wanna go /home. /

        So hoist up the John B's sails,
        See how the mainsail sets,
        Send for the captain ashore, let me go home;
        Let me go home, I wanna go home,
        I feel so lonesome, I wanna go home.

The captain's a wicked man,
He drinks whenever he can,
He don't give a damn 'bout grandaddy and me;
He kicks us around and shoves us about,
I feel so lonesome, I wanna go home.
(Chorus)

Well the first mate, he got drunk,
And destroyed the people's trunk,
The constable came aboard, took him away.
Let me alone, please let me alone,
I feel so lonesome, I wanna go home.
(Chorus)

MY BONNIE 3/4
Traditional

     D   G   D
My /Bonnie lies /over the /ocean, /

            G   A
My /Bonnie lies /over the /sea, /

     D   G   D
My /Bonnie lies /over the /ocean, /

       G   A   D
Oh, /bring back my /Bonnie to /me. /

  D   G
/Bring /back, oh, /bring /back,

     A   D
Oh, /bring back my /Bonnie to /me, to /me,

               G
/Bring /back, oh, /bring /back,

     A   D
Oh, /bring back my /Bonnie to /me. /

Oh, blow, ye winds, over the ocean,
Oh, blow, ye winds, over the sea.
Oh, blow, ye winds, over the ocean,
And bring back my Bonnie to me.

Last night as I lay on my pillow,
Last night as I lay on my bed,
Last night as I lay on my pillow,
I dreamed that my Bonnie was dead.

The winds have blown over the ocean,
The winds have blown over the sea,
The winds have blown over the ocean,
And brought back my Bonnie to me.

CLEMENTINE 3/4
Traditional

        D
In a /cavern, in a /canyon,

           A
Exca-/vating for a /mine,

                D
Lived a /miner, forty /niner,

      A   D
And his /daughter Clemen-/tine.

Oh my darling, oh my darling,
Oh my darling, Clementine,
You are lost and gone forever,
Dreadful sorry, Clementine.

Light she was and like a fairy,
And her shoes were number nine,
Herring boxes, without topses,
Sandals were for Clementine.

Drove she ducklings to the water,
Every morning just at nine,
Hit her foot against a splinter,
Fell into the foaming brine.

Ruby lips above the water,
Blowing bubbles soft and fine,
But alas I was no swimmer,
So I lost my Clementine.

There's a churchyard, on the hillside,
Where the flowers grow and twine,
There grow roses, 'mongst the posies,
Fertilized by Clementine.

BANKS OF THE OHIO 4/4
Traditional

          D   A
I asked my /love / – to take a /walk, /

                       D
To take a /walk, / – just a little /walk; /

                        G
Down be-/side / – where the waters /flow, /

            D   A   D
Down by the /banks / – of the Ohi-/o. /

And only say that you'll be mine,
In no other's arms entwined.
Down beside where the waters flow,
Down by the banks of the Ohio.

I held a knife against her breast
As gently in my arms she pressed.
She cried: "My love, don't you murder me,
I'm unprepared for eternity."

I wandered home 'tween twelve and one.
I cried: "My God, what have I done."
I killed the only girl I love,
Because she would not be my bride.

Key of G

G

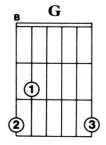

C

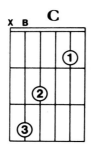

D

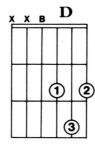

ON TOP OF OLD SMOKEY 3/4
Traditional

```
         G          C
On /top of old /Smo-/key, /

                  G
All /covered with /snow, / /

                   D
I /lost my true /lo-/ver, /

      D7          G
From /courting too /slow. / /
```

Now courting is pleasure
And parting is grief;
But a false-hearted lover,
Is worse than a thief.

A thief will just rob you
And take what you have,
But a false-hearted lover
Will lead you to the grave.

The grave will decay you
And turn you to dust,
Not one boy in a hundred
A poor girl can trust.

They'll hug you and kiss you
And tell you more lies
Than the cross-ties on a railroad,
Or stars in the skies.

Come all ye young maidens
And listen to me.
Never place your affection
On a green willow tree.

For the leaves they will wither
And the roots they will die.
You'll all be forsaken
And never know why.

MY GRANDFATHER'S CLOCK 4/4
Henry Clay Work

```
        G          D7       G          C
My /grandfather's /clock was too /large for the /shelf,

        G         D7          G
So it /stood ninety /years on the /floor; /

                   D7        G          C
It was /taller by /half than the /old man him-/self,

          G         D7          G
Though it /weighed not a /pennyweight /more. /

                             D7           G
It was /bought on the /morn of the /day he was /born,

                 A7          D7
And was /always his /treasure and /pride; /

          G      D7  G         C
But it /stopped /short, /never to go a-/gain

           G    D7  G
When the /old /man /died. /

            G
Ninety /years without /slumbering,

/Tick-tock, /tick-tock,

His /life's seconds /numbering,

/Tick-tock, /tick-tock,

           D7    G          C
And it /stopped /short, /never to go a-/gain

          G     D7  G
When the /old /man /died. /
```

In watching its pendulum swing to and fro,
Many an hour he spent as a boy.
And in childhood and manhood the clock seemed to know,
And to share both his grief and his joy.
For it struck twenty-four when he entered at the door,
With a blooming and beautiful bride;
But it stopped short, never to go again
When the old man died.
(Chorus)

My grandfather said that of those he could hire
Not a servant so faithful he found;
For it wasted no time, and had but one desire,
At the close of each week to be wound.
And it kept in its place, not a frown upon its face,
And its hands never hung by its side, etc.
(Chorus)

Key of E

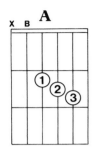

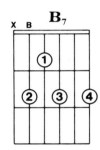

I USED TO PLAY   3/4
Traditional

```
    E              A
I /used to /play my /old ban-/jo

    E          B₇
And /sing a /song to /you; /

    E              A
But /now the /strings are /broken,

    E    B₇    E
/So I /cannot /sing to /you. /
```

I took it to a mender's shop
To see what they could do.
But still the strings are broken,
So I cannot sing to you.

I came into the room last night,
they sang a song, cocoo.
The broken strings I mind no more;
I now can sing to you.

AMAZING GRACE   3/4
Traditional

```
    E              A      E
A-/mazing /grace, how /sweet the /sound

                      B₇
That /saved a /wretch like /me. /

    E          A      E
I /once was /lost, but /now am /found;

         B₇   E
Was /blind, but /now I /see. /
```

'Twas grace that taught my heart to fear,
And grace my fears relieved.
How precious did that grace appear,
The hour I first believed.

Through many dangers, toils and snares,
I have already come;
'Tis grace that brought me safe thus far,
And grace will lead me home.

When we've been there ten thousand years,
Bright shining as the sun;
We've no less days to sing God's praise
Than when we first begun.

MIDNIGHT SPECIAL   4/4
Traditional

```
    E              A
/Well you wake up in the /morning, /

                      E
Hear the work bell /ring, /

                          B₇
You go a-marching to the /table, /

                    E
You see the same old /thing; /

                        A
Ain't no food upon the /table, /

                  E
Just an egg in a /pan, /

                      B₇
But you better not com-/plain boy, /

                          E
You'll get in trouble with the /man. /

                    A
Let the midnight /special /

                      E
Shine her light on /me; /

                    B₇
Let the midnight /special /

                        E
Shine her ever-loving /light on me. /
```

If you ever go to Houston,
You better walk right;
You better not gamble,
You better not fight;
Sheriff Benson will arrest you,
His men will drag you down,
The next thing you know boy,
You see you're prison bound.
(Chorus)

Yonder comes little Rosie,
How in the world do you know?
I can tell her by her apron,
And the clothes she wore.
Umbrella on her shoulder,
Piece of paper in her hand,
She goes a-marching to the warden,
Says: "Please release my man."
(Chorus)

31

Key of C

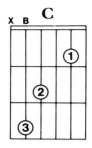

C

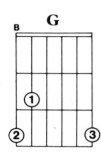

G

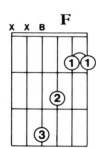

F

To play the F chord, you have to depress two strings with one finger. This means that you cannot just use the tip of your finger. You have to actually press the ball of your finger flat against the strings.

To start with, press your first finger down on the two strings until you can get both strings to sound clear. Make sure that your finger is pressing right behind the fret. When you feel confident about this part of the chord, put your second and third fingers on their strings. You can lower your thumb so that it presses directly opposite your first finger.

WHEN THE SAINTS GO MARCHING IN   4/4
Traditional

```
                    C
Oh, when the /saints /go marching /in, /

                                    G₇
Oh, when the /saints go /marching /in, /

          C           F
I want to /be /in that /number, /

          C        G₇     C
When the /saints go /marching /in. /
```

Oh, when the new world is revealed, etc.
And when the revelation comes, etc.
Oh, when they gather 'round the throne, etc.
And when they crown Him King of Kings, etc.
And on that hallelujah day, etc.

THE GYPSY ROVER 4/4
Traditional

```
       C    G₇      C       G₇
The /gypsy /rover came /over the /hill,

       C              G₇      C G₇
/Bound through the /valley so /sha-/dy;

       C             G₇        Em      Am
He /whistled and he /sang till the /green woods /rang,

       Em         Dm        C F C  G₇
And /he won the /heart of a /la/-a-/dy. /

       C    G₇     C     G₇
/Ha di /do, ah di /do da /day,

       C    G₇     C    G₇
/Ah di /do, ah di /day /dee;

              C       G₇        Em      Am
He /whistled and he /sang till the /green woods /rang,

       Em         Dm        C F C  G₇
And /he won the /heart of a /la/-a-/dy. /
```

She left her father's castle gate,
She left her own true lover;
She left her servants and her estate,
To follow the gypsy rover.
(Chorus)

Her father saddled his fastest steed,
Roamed the valley all over;
Sought his daughter at great speed,
And the whistling gypsy rover.
(Chorus)

He came at last to a mansion fine,
Down by the river Clyde;
And there was music and there was wine,
For the gypsy and his lady.
(Chorus)

He's no gypsy, my father, she said,
My lord of freelands all over;
and I will stay till my dying day,
With my whistling gypsy rover.
(Chorus)

The capo

A capo is a small device that is fitted around the neck of the guitar in order to raise the pitch of all the strings.

When, for instance, you fit a capo behind the second fret and finger the C chord, you will actually be playing the D chord (which is two semitones higher than C).

Each singer has a certain range within which he can sing comfortably. Some songs may be in a key that is not within your range. By experimenting with a capo in different positions, you can easily change the key of a song to one that is better suited to your voice, without changing any of the chords.

There is a wide variety of capos to choose from, all of which work more

or less equally well. Just make sure that the one you buy fits your fingerboard. Classical guitars usually have flat fingerboards, while those of steel-string guitars are usually slightly rounded.

The main disadvantage of a capo is that it tends to pull the strings out of tune. For this reason, many guitarists

choose the capo with the elastic band – this is also usually the cheapest.

After fastening the capo around the neck of the guitar, push it forward – away from the strings. Any string that has been pulled out of tune will then return to normal. If you do this, you will find that the capo does not interfere with the tuning of your guitar.

You can make a makeshift capo using half a pencil and a couple of elastic bands.

The capo can also be used to produce specific effects, since it makes the guitar sound generally higher and brighter. Players of traditional kwela music, in particular, favour this sound.

Bar chords

Bar chords are the key to the rest of the chords on the guitar. By using only a few simple chord patterns, you can play just about any chord imaginable on the guitar.

The name "bar chord" is derived from the position of the first finger, which forms a bar across all the strings, as if replacing the nut at the top of the fretboard. Next to the bar, the other fingers form normal chord patterns.

Bar chords are movable chord patterns. The whole pattern can be moved either up or down the fretboard to form different chords.

The most commonly used bar chords are those using the E and A chord patterns.

BAR CHORDS WITH THE E PATTERN

To free the first finger so that it can be used to form the bar, the normal E chord must be fingered with the second, third and fourth fingers.

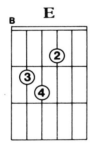

E

Now move the chord pattern up one fret and place the first finger across all six strings behind the first fret. You are now fingering the F chord.

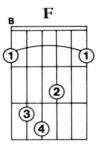

F

Each fret on the fretboard represents a semitone. This means that each time the chord pattern is moved up one fret, the chord as a whole becomes one semitone higher.

BASS ROOT

The bass root of the chord you have just learnt is the sixth string fingered with the first finger. The position of the bass root determines the name of the chord.

This means that, in many cases, you have to know only the notes on the sixth string in order to decide where to finger the chord pattern to play a certain chord.

Most guitars have guide dots at the fifth and seventh frets. Start by learning the notes at these frets. You can then work out the rest of the notes according to the guide dots.

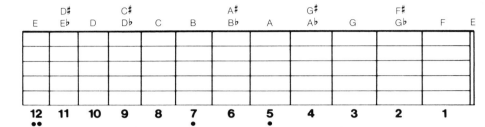

E	D♯ E♭	D	C♯ D♭	C	B	A♯ B♭	A	G♯ A♭	G	F♯ G♭	F	E
12	11	10	9	8	7	6	5	4	3	2	1	

Bass root

MINOR AND SEVENTH CHORDS

The minor and seventh chords also use the patterns of the E chord.

If you form the Em chord with your third and fourth fingers, move the whole pattern up one fret and form a bar with your first finger behind the first fret. You will then be fingering the Fm chord.

Fm

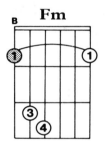 

F₇

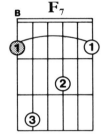 

Examples

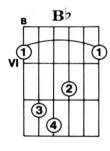 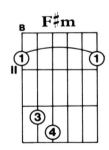 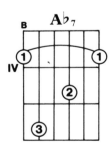

The Roman numeral indicates the fret where the chord should be fingered.

ALTERNATIVE CHORD

F

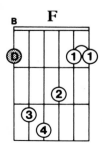 

There is also another way to finger the major chord, which is particularly favoured by players with steel-string guitars. The first finger forms a half-bar across the first two strings and the sixth string is depressed by the thumb. This is a very effective way to finger the F chord, especially when it is used with the C chord.

BAR CHORDS WITH THE A PATTERN

As with the E chord, the A chord must be fingered with the second, third and fourth fingers so as to free the first finger to form a bar.

Move the chord pattern up one fret and place the first finger across the first five strings (or all six if you find it easier) behind the first fret. The chord you are now fingering is B♭.

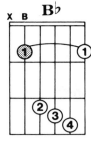

The bass root of this chord pattern is the fifth string, fingered with the first finger.

It is, therefore, necessary to know the notes on the fifth string in order to be able to decide where to finger the A chord pattern to form a certain chord.

A	G# / A♭	G	F# / G♭	F	E	D# / E♭	D	C# / D♭	C	B	B♭	A
12	11	10	9	8	7	6	5	4	3	2	1	

MINOR CHORDS

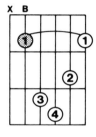

SEVENTH CHORDS

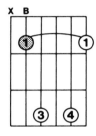

Examples

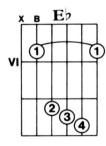

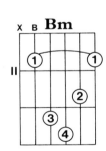

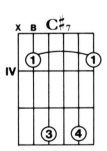

ALTERNATIVE CHORD

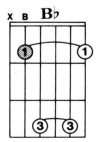

The major chord can also be played by forming a half-bar across the fourth, third and second strings.

Transposing

When a song is in a key that is either too high or too low for you to sing it comfortably, you can transpose it to a key that is better suited to your voice.

It is quite simple to transpose a song: write down the chords of the song in alphabetical order, starting with the main chord of the key.

For example, when a song is in the key of G it will look like this:

G A B C D E F♯

Beneath these chords, write down the chords of the new key in alphabetical order.

Suppose you want to transpose the song to the key of C (each key's sharp and flat signs are discussed in the chapter on melody):

G A B C D E F♯
C E F♯ G A B C♯

Now replace each chord in the song with the chord that is written underneath, for example, all the D chords in the old key will become G chords in the new key.

Note that every minor or seventh chord in the old key should also be a minor or seventh chord in the new key.

Example

Old key

$\quad$ G $\qquad\qquad$ Em
Where have all the flowers gone,
$\quad$ C $\qquad$ D
Long time passing?
$\quad$ G $\qquad\qquad$ Em
Where have all the flowers gone,
$\quad$ C $\qquad$ D$_7$
Long time ago?

New key

$\quad$ C $\qquad\qquad$ Am
Where have all the flowers gone,
$\quad$ F $\qquad$ G
Long time passing?
$\quad$ C $\qquad\qquad$ Am
Where have all the flowers gone,
$\quad$ F $\qquad$ G$_7$
Long time ago?

Additional chords

Alternative chords

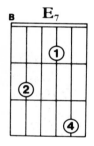 E$_7$

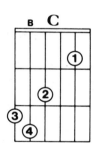 C

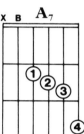 A$_7$

Suspended fourths

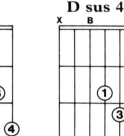 D sus 4 / A sus 4

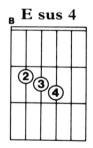 E sus 4

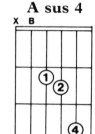 (C sus 4)

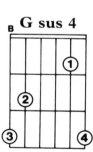 G sus 4

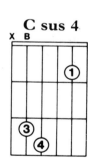 C sus 4

Jazz chords

Jazz guitarists mostly use movable chord patterns. These are similar to bar chords in the sense that a particular pattern can be fingered at different places on the fretboard in order to form different chords.

As in the case of bar chords, the bass root determines where the pattern must be fingered to form a certain chord. On the diagrams, the bass roots are indicated by the darkened circles.

In jazz chords, certain strings in the middle of some chords should not be played – these strings are marked with an X. To prevent a string from sounding, touch it lightly with a neighbouring finger. Alternatively, play the bass string with your thumb and pluck the rest of the strings with your fingers.

A Roman numeral indicates the fret at which the chord should be fingered.

To familiarise yourself with the chords, experiment with the following chord sequences:

1. /Cmaj$_7$ /A$_7$ /Dm$_7$ /G$_7$ //

2. /Gmaj$_7$ /Em$_7$ /A$_9$ /Dm$_7$ //

3. /F /Fmaj$_7$ /C$_7$ /F$_7$ /B♭$_7$ /A$_7$ /F //

4. /G /Am$_7$ /Bm /D$_7$ /G /Am$_7$ /Bm /Am$_7$ /
/G /Am$_7$ /G /B$_7$ /E /A /E /A /E /A /C♯ /C♯ D /G //

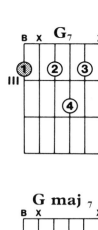

G₇   Seventh

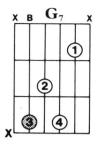

G₇

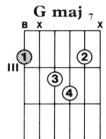

G maj ₇   Major seventh

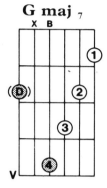

G maj ₇

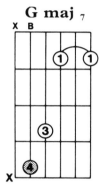

G maj ₇

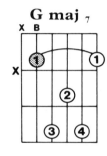

G maj ₇

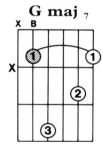

G maj ₇

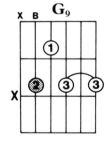

G₉   Ninth

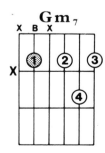

Gm ₇   Minor seventh

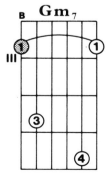

Gm ₇

37

Diminished chord

Diminished chords can be named after any of the notes in the chord. The chord in the diagram could therefore be D⁰, F⁰, B⁰ or G⁰. These four notes are repeated each time the chord is moved up three frets; the chord can, therefore, be played at several different places on the fretboard.

D⁰

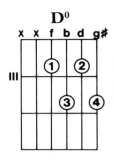

Chord sequences

Thousands of hit songs have been written using only the three basic chords of a key. The possibilities of this formula have still not been exhausted, and fresh, original songs based only on three primary chords of a key are still being written.

There are a number of other popular chord combinations on which a great many songs have been based. A good example is the sequence Am G F E. More examples are listed alongside.

Try experimenting with the different sequences. Each sequence can be repeated over and over again, and is written in such a way that each chord lasts for one bar, but you certainly don't have to stick rigidly to this. Remember that original and innovative work generally stems from the ability to ignore set rules and to improvise.

Have you ever tried to compose a song? It's really not *that* difficult to make a start. One way is to play a chord sequence that you like over and over again and then hum a tune to it.

To put words to this tune, you must just have an idea of what you want the song to be about. Try out a few lines that fit the melody and work on these until you have a full verse.

You can use a different chord sequence for the chorus. The chorus is generally more melodious than the verse and usually features the catch-line of the song – one line that says in a nutshell what the song is about. In-

stead of composing your song on a re-petitive chord sequence, try to write the catch-line first, with the rest of the song around it.

The chord sequences listed here can also be used when learning the various strumming and fingerpicking patterns discussed at the end of the next chapter.

There are unlimited possible combinations of rhythm patterns and chord sequences. However, instead of trying as many different combinations as possible, concentrate rather on one sequence at a time and explore the possibilities that this particular sequence has to offer.

```
/C /F /G /F //
/C /G /Am /Am //
/C /F /G /G //
/C /Am /F /G //
/C /Am /Dm /G //
/C /F /C /F /G /G //
/C /G /F /G //

/Am /G /F /E //
/Am /Dm /Am /E //
/Am /F /G /Am //
/Am /G /F /F //
/Am /C /G /Am //
/Am /G /G /Am //

/G /D /C /C //
/G /Em /C /D //
/G /C /D /C //
```

```
/G /C /G /C /D /D //
/G /Am /D /C //
/G /C /D /D₇ //
/G /Bm /C /D //

/Em /D /C /Em //
/Em /Am /Em /Am //
/Em /G /D /Em //
/Em /Bm /C /D //
/Em /D /C /G //
/Em /C /D /D //

/D /A /G /A //
/D /Bm /G /A /A //
/D /G /A /G //
/D /C /G /G //
/D /A /Bm /G /D /A /D /D //
/D /A /G /G //

/Bm /G /A /Bm //
/Bm /Bm /E /E //
/Bm /Bm /G /A //

/A /D /E /A //
/A /E /D /D //
/A /F♯m /D /E //
/A /D /E /A /F♯m /Bm /D /E //

/E /A /E /A /E /A /B₇ /B₇ //
/E /E /D /A //
/E /C♯m /F♯m /F♯m /B₇ /B₇ /E /E //
/E /A /E /B //
/E /E /F♯m /F♯m /A /A /E /E //

/Dm /Dm /C /C //
/Dm /F /C /C //
/Dm /Am /F /G //
/Dm /F /C /G //
```

4 RHYTHM

Playing regularly

To play a song well, you must be able to play it fluently and rhythmically. Although in time you will develop a natural sense of rhythm, this is something which must be practised regularly and frequently in the beginning.

Get into the habit of picking up your guitar every single day. If you resolve to play at least once a day, this will soon become a way of life. With regular practise, you will eventually develop natural tempo, accent and feeling.

You don't have to learn something new every day. You should rather practise pieces you have already learnt so that your playing will become fluent and polished.

Rhythm is the source of energy and movement in music. Strive to enjoy the rhythm in your music so that you can draw energy from it when you are practising.

Triple and quadruple time

In Western music, there are two main types of rhythm: triple time and quadruple time.

Triple time has three beats per bar and is counted "*one*, two, three; *one*, two, three". This is also known as the waltz rhythm.

Quadruple time, otherwise known as four-four time, has four beats per bar and is counted "one, two, three, four; one, two, three, four".

To get a visual image of triple time, think of a group of people sitting next to each other singing, while swaying from side to side in time to the music. On the first count, which is accented and should thus be the loudest, the people sway over to one side. On the second and third counts, they remain still. On the first count of the next

bar, they sway back to the other side again. *One*, two, three; *one* two, three. Try to feel the rhythm by swaying from side to side while counting the beat.

Quadruple time can be compared to steady, even footsteps. In contrast to triple time, which is a swaying rhythm, quadruple time is a pulsing, pounding rhythm. There is also no hard and fast rule about where the accent should fall in quadruple time. Which beat is accentuated differs according to the type of music. In rock music, for example, the accent falls on the first and third beat. In reggae, on the other hand, the second and fourth beats are accentuated. In most modern music, all four beats are accentuated, and this is why this type of

music has such a pulsing rhythm.

When you listen to music, try tapping the beat with your hand. Do not concentrate on the more intricate rhythms – just the even pulse of the music. Also note the function of the accent in different kinds of music.

Strumming

Strumming is a rhythmical stroking of all the guitar strings, using the thumb, index finger or a plectrum.

You can start strumming by playing the rhythm with the nail of your index finger. (You will use exactly the same action when you eventually start using a plectrum. In fact, the plectrum becomes an extension of your index finger. But more about this later.)

In order to have better control over

your index finger, you can support it with your thumb. Play downwards so that the nail of your index finger hits the strings.

TRIPLE TIME STRUMMING
Triple time gets its character from the accent on the first beat of the bar.

Finger a chord. Count "one, two, three; one, two, three" while strumming the strings once for each count.

Now play with an accent, that is, louder on the first count of each bar. To make the accent stronger, play only the three thin strings on the sec-ond and third counts. In other words, on the first count play loudly across all the strings, and on the second and third counts, play softly over the three thin strings – loud, soft, soft; loud, soft, soft.

Practise this waltz strumming until you can manage to play it with an even rhythm. Then try it with all the other chords you know. (Remember not to play the sixth string of the A and C chords or the fifth and sixth strings of the D chord.) Also practise changing chords while you are strumming.

Now try playing the songs marked 3/4 in the previous chapter using triple time strumming.

FOUR-FOUR STRUMMING
In contrast to triple time strumming, where there is always a distinct accent on the first beat of the bar, in basic four-four strumming there is an accent on each of the four beats.

Finger a chord and count "one, two, three, four; one, two, three, four" while strumming once across the strings for each count.

To bring out the character of four-four strumming, try playing only the bass strings on the first and third counts, and only the treble strings on the second and fourth counts. None of the beats should be any louder than the others. Each beat should be accentuated, just like steady footsteps.

In other words, play as follows: bass strings, treble strings, bass strings, treble strings. Try this out with the chords you know, and then learn to play a few songs in four-four time using this method of strumming.

Nails and plectrums
THE NAILS OF YOUR RIGHT HAND
When guitar strings are plucked with the fleshy part of your fingertips only, a soft, weak sound is produced. A better sound can be produced by letting your nails grow just past your fingertips. Keep your nails at a comfortable length, however – long enough to catch the strings when you play, but not so long that you pluck the strings with your nails only.

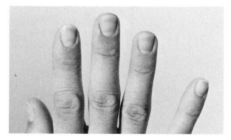

You will get the best sound if you pluck the string with the tip of your finger, then letting the nail strike the string briefly. Experiment with this.

Don't use nail hardener if your nails break easily. It will not only make them hard, but brittle as well. And brittle nails have a tendency to break. Rather rub some baby oil on them from time to time. This is not only good for your nails, it also makes them strong and slightly pliable, which will prevent them from breaking too easily.

Use a nail-file to keep your nails smooth and the right length.

The guitar as a drum
Playing along with records is excellent exercise for your right hand when you are learning to strum. The problem is that you will not know the chords of each song. This can be overcome easily, by using your guitar as a drum.

A drum has no identifiable pitch. It produces only the rhythm, without notes or chords. If you deaden the strings of your guitar so that you can hear only the percussion, your guitar will become equivalent to a drum.

Hold your left hand lightly over the strings, more or less where the neck meets the body of the guitar. This will prevent the strings from vibrating freely and producing an identifiable pitch.

Now you can play along to your heart's content with any record, concentrating only on the rhythm, without bothering with the chords.

You should play only to the beat

of the music at first, until you can play an even rhythm with your right hand. When you feel comfortable with this new technique, start experimenting. Try to add extra strumming where this sounds right. It is good practice to repeat *one* song over and over again – the more you hear it, the easier it becomes to play a fitting rhythm.

It can be great fun to play the rhythm of the songs you like. And even if you just keep on repeating the same rhythm, this is still excellent exercise for your right hand.

PLECTRUMS

Plectrums come in all shapes and sizes, and can be hard or soft, large or small, and made of plastic, nylon or hard rubber. A guitarist will usually select a particular plectrum after he has experimented with an assortment of different ones.

Thin, flexible plectrums give a light, crisp sound and are good for very fast strumming. Hard, stiff plectrums give a rounder, more solid sound with a strong bass.

You must choose the plectrum that suits *you* best. Experiment until you find the one that is perfect for you.

Hold the plectrum between your thumb and index finger in such a way that only the tip of the plectrum protrudes past the tip of your index finger. The plectrum should, in fact, feel like an extension of this finger.

THUMB AND FINGER-PICKS
Many folk-singers use thumb-picks to enable them to play a strong rhythm on the bass strings.

The thumb-pick fits around the thumb with the flat side at the bottom. If the thumb-pick is either too loose or too tight around the thumb, heat the curve with a match and pull it open or press it tighter until it fits comfortably.

If your nails are very soft or tend to break easily, you can pluck the strings using one or two finger-picks. These are not as easy to use as thumb-picks, but with a little practise you should be able to get the hang of it.

Finger-picks are sometimes used to produce a particular sound, for instance in kwela music, where the up-beat is generally accentuated.

Make sure that the part that strikes the strings is the part pressed against the fleshy side of the fingertip – the strings should be plucked by the rounded side of the pick.

Development of four-four strumming

From basic four-four strumming you can now develop quite a few variations that will make your strumming more interesting and versatile.

For the next exercise, play a very simple chord sequence. I would suggest that you play the G chord for two bars, then Am for two bars, then G again for two, and so on.

In tablature, basic four-four strumming will look as follows (the bass strings are at the bottom; the arrows thus indicate that you should play downward strokes):

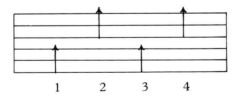

Play the pattern for two bars on G, then two on Am, and then back to G again. Try from the start to play with a good flowing rhythm that is neither too fast nor too slow. Remember not to play the sixth string of the Am chord. Now try a simplified version of the pattern using four even downward strokes only:

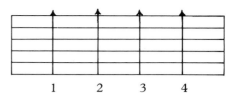

The next step is to start playing upward as well as downward strokes. To loosen your wrist, start by playing downward and upward strokes in no particularly recognisable pattern:

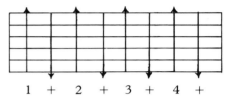

Now combine the two patterns. Play G and Am for a couple of bars using only downward strokes, and then change to downward *and* upward strokes without slowing down. You may find this a little difficult at first, but keep on trying until you can do it.

When you can do this well, try to reduce the number of strokes:

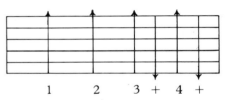

You need not play *all* the strings with each stroke. For example, try strumming the bass strings only for the first two strokes and then the treble strings only for the rest of the strokes:

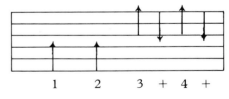

Vary this pattern every now and then by playing a couple of bars with strokes on the first and third counts only:

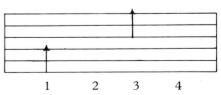

While playing a bar with strokes on the first and third counts (still keeping the main pattern in mind), it should not be too difficult to add an unexpected upward stroke:

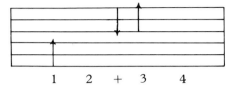

Try to add upward strokes elsewhere too:

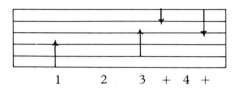

Now put an accent on each of the ringed strokes:

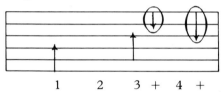

If you got lost along the way, start again. It is unlikely that you will be able to go through the entire process in one go. Take one step at a time and practise it until it becomes a natural action. It is definitely worth the effort to work through the whole process, as it will enable you to play just about any strumming pattern you can imagine. Experiment to achieve different effects. Accentuate different strokes and try to find the most effective places to play upward strokes.

Fingerpicking

Fingerpicking is the act of plucking the strings with the fingers in a certain pattern. The classical term for this is arpeggio, derived from the Italian word *arpa*, which means harp – the strings are plucked in the same way as a harp is played.

Each finger on your right hand has a name. To distinguish them from the

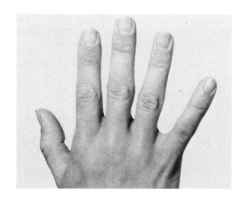

fingers of your left hand, they are not referred to as first, second and third fingers. Instead, the fingers of the right hand are usually referred to by the letters p, i, m and a:

p = thumb (p stands for *pulgar*, Spanish for thumb)
i = index finger (*indice* – to point)
m = middle finger (*medio* – middle)
a = ring finger (*anular* – ring)

(The little finger is not named because it is not used in fingerpicking.)

A FINGERPICKING PATTERN

Place your fingers on the strings as in the photo: the thumb on the sixth string, the index finger on the second string and the middle finger on the first string.

While holding the index and middle fingers on their strings, try playing a steady rhythm on the sixth string with your thumb.

The thumb plays downwards, and the other fingers upwards. Play the following pattern with your right hand, without fingering a chord with your left hand.

a The thumb (p) plays the sixth string.
b The index finger (i) plays the second string.
c The middle finger (m) plays the first string.
d The index finger plays the second string again.

When you repeat this pattern, it should form one long, rhythmic whole. You should not, therefore,

Tablature

Tablature for the guitar is written on six lines, which represent the six strings. The bottom line represents the thickest string, and the top line the thinnest string.

Thinnest string

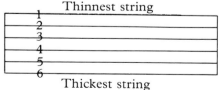

Thickest string
To write a fingerpicking pattern in tablature, the chord is written

at the top and the name of the finger that plucks each string is written on the relevant line.

This is the tablature of the fingerpicking pattern described above:

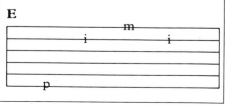

pause after the fourth note, but should immediately play the sixth string again with the thumb. Try to maintain an even rhythm.

You will have to concentrate very hard at this stage to make sure each finger plays the correct string, but if you practise regularly, this should soon come naturally.

It will help a lot if you hold your guitar in the classical position so that your right hand is not needed to keep your guitar in position. Ensure that your thumb is slightly in front of your other fingers, as in the photo. Your fingers should form a diagonal line across the strings so that each finger can move unhindered.

Fingerpicking to a song

In the beginning, it might seem impossible to play a fingerpicking pattern and sing at the same time. The solution is to know the pattern so well and feel so comfortable with it that you hardly have to concentrate on playing it and can, therefore, focus most of your attention on your singing. If you practise often enough, fingerpicking will come naturally.

Try to play a strong, steady beat with your thumb. The other strings should merely complement the bass strings and should be subordinate to the thumb's rhythm.

When you are quite familiar with the two fingerpicking patterns, use them to play some of the songs in the previous chapter.

TRIPLE TIME
FINGERPICKING

Basic pattern
E

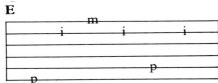

Key of A
A

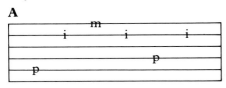

D

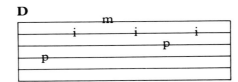

E

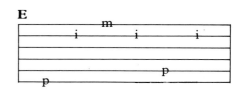

Key of G
G

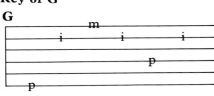

C

D

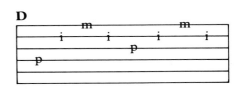

FOUR-FOUR FINGERPICKING

Basic pattern
E

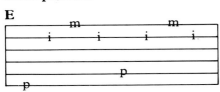

Key of A
A

D

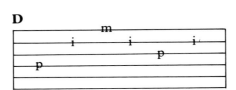

E

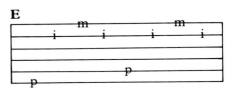

Key of G
G

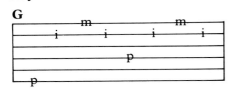

C

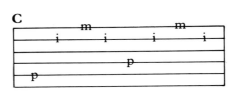

D

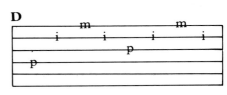

43

Bass roots

Every normal major or minor chord is made up of three notes. Look, for example, at the following chords:

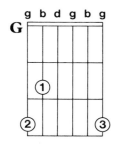

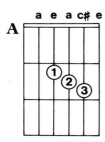

As you can see, the C chord consists of the notes c e g; G consists of g b d;

and A of a c♯ e. Theoretically, a chord is made up of the first, third and fifth notes built on the root of the chord, for instance:

C = ⓒ d ⓔ f ⓖ

G = ⓖ a ⓑ c ⓓ

A = ⓐ b ⓒ♯ d ⓔ

The root of a chord is the note with the same name as the chord. This also forms the foundation of the chord and is, therefore, the most important note.

The bass root is the lowest root formed in a chord. For instance, in the C chord, the lowest C note is formed by depressing the fifth string behind the third fret. This note is the bass root of the C chord.

The bass roots of the basic chords are as follows:

G G₇ E Em E₇   – sixth string
C C₇ A Am A₇ B₇   – fifth string
D D₇ Dm F   – fourth string

Note that the bass root of the E chord is an E note, that of the G chord is a G note, and that of the D chord is the unfingered fourth string – a D note. In other words, the bass root of each chord is a note with the same name as

the chord. This should be obvious from the diagram below. If you study this diagram you will see that you can actually work out what the bass root of each chord will be.

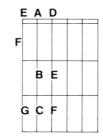

The string that is the bass root of each chord is also indicated on the chord diagrams in the previous chapter.

The bass root of each chord plays an important part in strumming and fingerpicking. It is this string that will carry most of the accent in any strumming or fingerpicking pattern.

The strumming and fingerpicking patterns on the next three pages are meant for the G chord only. The first note of each pattern is usually the bass root of G – the sixth string. To play the same pattern for another chord, play the bass root of that particular chord. For instance, where you would usually play the sixth string for the G chord, you should now play the fourth string for the D chord.

Strumming and fingerpicking patterns

Although the following strumming and fingerpicking patterns form the basic rhythms of thousands of songs, they can still be used in new and original ways.

As was the case with the chord sequences at the end of the previous chapter, you are free to do whatever you want with the following patterns.

Concentrate on only one pattern at a time and experiment with it. Remember that what is written here is only the basic pattern – the way *you* interpret it is what is really important.

When you become familiar with a basic pattern, break away and add something different: play it more slowly or chase the beat, play it with

an exaggerated accent on certain counts or make it soft and dreamy . . .

Rhythm is the life-energy of music.

As you get to know the different patterns, you will develop a feeling for which patterns are best suited to which songs.

STRUMMING PATTERNS: 3/4

G

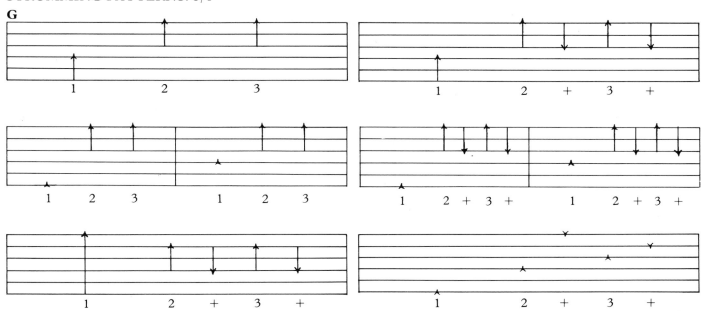

STRUMMING PATTERNS: 4/4

G

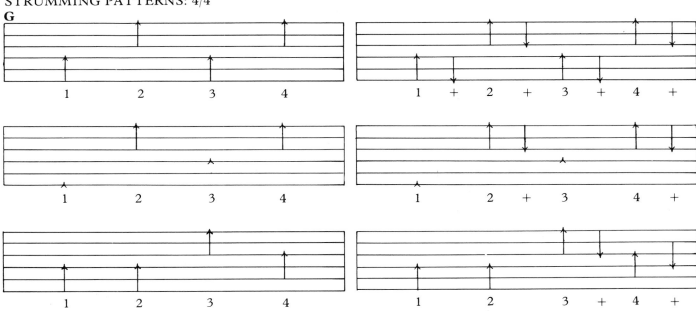

Folk

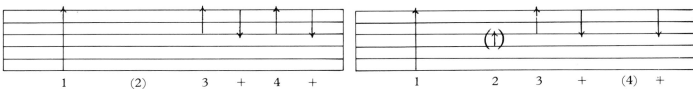

Rock

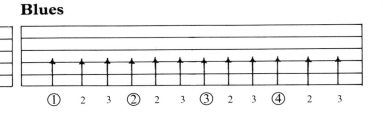

$$\text{①} \quad + \quad 2 \quad + \quad \text{③} \quad + \quad 4$$

Blues

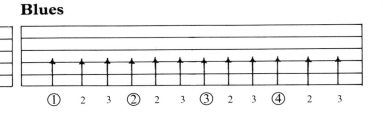

$$\text{①} \quad 2 \quad 3 \quad \text{②} \quad 2 \quad 3 \quad \text{③} \quad 2 \quad 3 \quad \text{④} \quad 2 \quad 3$$

Shuffle

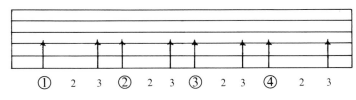

$$\text{①} \quad 2 \quad 3 \quad \text{②} \quad 2 \quad 3 \quad \text{③} \quad 2 \quad 3 \quad \text{④} \quad 2 \quad 3$$

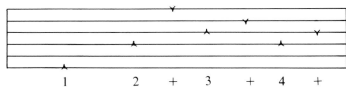

$$1 \quad 2 \quad + \quad 3 \quad + \quad 4 \quad +$$

FINGERPICKING PATTERNS: 3/4

G

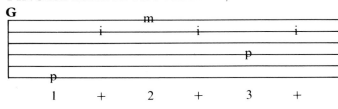

$$1 \quad + \quad 2 \quad + \quad 3 \quad +$$

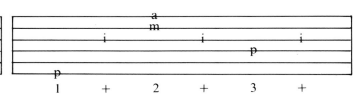

$$1 \quad + \quad 2 \quad + \quad 3 \quad +$$

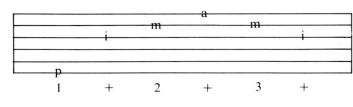

$$1 \quad + \quad 2 \quad + \quad 3 \quad +$$

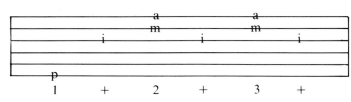

$$1 \quad + \quad 2 \quad + \quad 3 \quad +$$

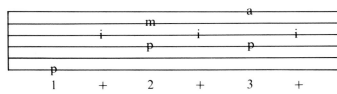

$$1 \quad + \quad 2 \quad + \quad 3 \quad +$$

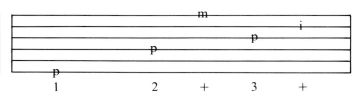

$$1 \quad 2 \quad + \quad 3 \quad +$$

FINGERPICKING PATTERNS: 4/4

G

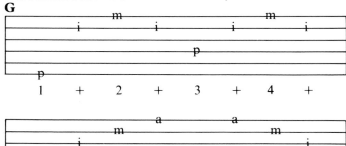

$$1 \quad + \quad 2 \quad + \quad 3 \quad + \quad 4 \quad +$$

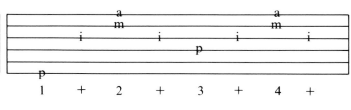

$$1 \quad + \quad 2 \quad + \quad 3 \quad + \quad 4 \quad +$$

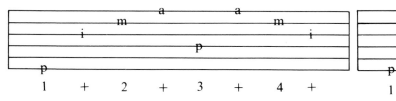

$$1 \quad + \quad 2 \quad + \quad 3 \quad + \quad 4 \quad +$$

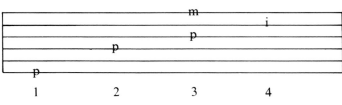

$$1 \quad 2 \quad 3 \quad 4$$

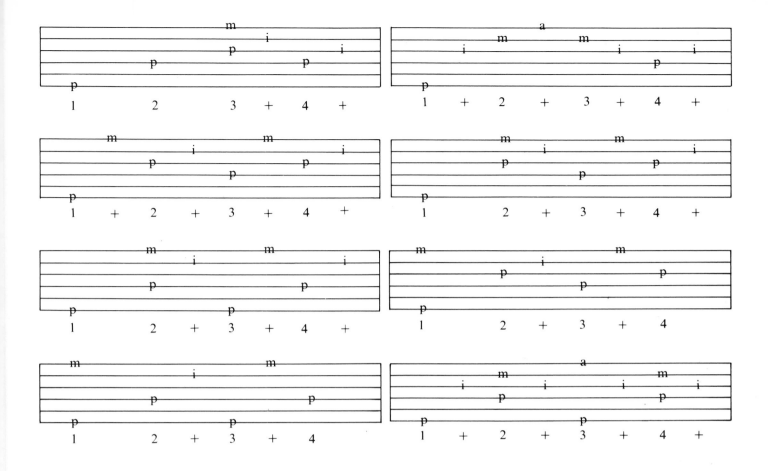

5 MELODY

Improvisation

In modern music, the lead guitarist usually improvises on the basic melody of a song. This improvisation is loosely based on the original melody, but the guitarist then creates a more interesting and faster solo piece, generally called a "lead break", by adding series of notes derived from the scale in which the music is written.

To be able to improvise like this, you need to know your scales and to develop a feeling for melody.

Melody by ear

The best way to develop a feeling for melody is to learn to play melodies by ear.

Playing by ear requires ear-hand coordination, since the idea is to play what you hear in your head. On the other hand, to be able to play a melody following written music requires eye-hand coordination – you play what you read.

This does not mean that sight-reading is bad. On the contrary, sight-reading has many advantages, but to learn to play music by sight-reading *only* can inhibit the natural development of your musical ear.

To develop your musical sense, make a point of playing by ear rather than limiting yourself to written music. This will also develop your ability to compose melodies and music, and to improvise on a set piece of music.

Start to work out melodies by ear by playing on one string only. Do not worry about the names of the notes.

Just let your ear guide you. You might find this a little difficult in the beginning, but after you have worked out the first part of the tune, the next part will be easier. It definitely helps if you start with simple melodies you know well.

You need not work out each song's complete melody. Try a phrase from one song, and then part of another. The purpose of the exercise is to coordinate the tune you hear in your head and the notes you play on your guitar.

The sharp and flat signs of a key

At one time or another you have probably wondered how the sharp and flat notes in a key are determined.

Try this experiment:
Play the note that is formed when you depress the second string behind the first fret. This note is C. If you play

the second string behind the thirteenth fret, you will again play C, but an octave higher.

Try to work out the scale of C for yourself, from the first to the thirteenth fret – it should sound like Do, Re, Mi, Fa, So, La, Ti, Do. Let your ear guide you as to when you should move one fret at a time, and when you should move two.

Also play backwards from the thirteenth to the first fret. Now work out the entire scale before you read any further.

The scale should look like this:

Scale of C

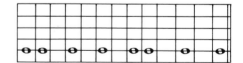

If you now play the same pattern on any of the other strings, it will still sound correct. On the fourth string, for instance, you will be playing the scale of E♭. As you can see this pattern applies to all major scales.

Each key's sharp and flat signs ensure that the key keeps to this pattern.

Major keys	Relative minor keys
C – 0	Am
G – 1 – f♯	Em
D – 2 – f♯ c♯	Bm
A – 3 – f♯ c♯ g♯	F♯m
E – 4 – f♯ c♯ g♯ d♯	C♯m
B – 5 – f♯ c♯ g♯ d♯ e♯	G♯m
F – 1 – b♭	Dm
B♭ – 2 – b♭ e♭	Gm
E♭ – 3 – b♭ e♭ a♭	Cm
A♭ – 4 – b♭ e♭ a♭ d♭	Fm
D♭ – 5 – b♭ e♭ a♭ d♭ g♭	B♭m
G♭ – 6 – b♭ e♭ a♭ d♭ g♭ c♭	E♭m

Can you see that strange but obvious patterns are formed in the list on the left? The diagram below is a handy guide to help you work out each key's sharp and flat signs. Try to figure out the principle behind this diagram and how the diagram should be used.

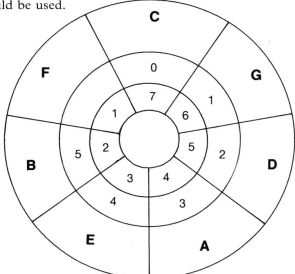

MINOR KEYS
Each minor key is related to a specific major key, and takes the sharps and flats of that major key. The key of B minor, for instance, is related to the key of D major and, therefore, has two sharps: F♯ and C♯.

Tablature

As mentioned in the previous chapter, tablature is a simple way to write down music for string instruments. Tablature for the guitar is written on six lines, which represent the six strings of the guitar.

The bottom line represents the thickest string, and the top line the thinnest string.

The numbers written on the lines indicate behind which fret the string should be depressed.

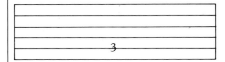

An open or unfingered string which should be played is indicated by a nought.

A string which is unmarked, however, should not be played at all.

The chord to be fingered is written at the top of the staff.

Underneath the staff, the right-hand fingering is indicated.

When the rhythm is simple and even, the length of the notes is not usually indicated.

Melodies for practice

For practice, and in order to get to know the notes of the different keys, try to work out the tunes on the next two pages. Only the first phrase of each song is given. You must work out the rhythm and the rest of the song by yourself.

If you get stuck, whistle or sing the tune to refresh your memory.

The songs are divided into keys to help you familiarise yourself with the notes of each key.

KEY OF C

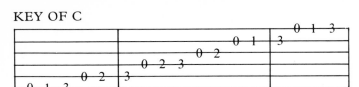

E F G A B C D E F G A B C D E F G

Oh, Susanna

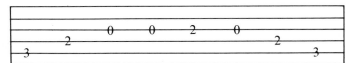

The gypsy rover

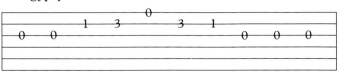

KEY OF G

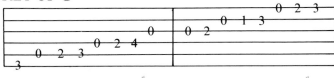

G A B C D E F♯G   G A B C D E F♯G

Silent night, Holy night

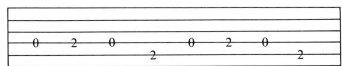

My grandfather's clock

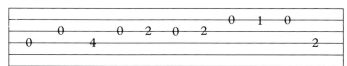

Where have all the flowers gone?

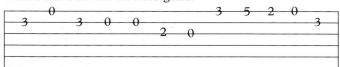

On top of old Smokey

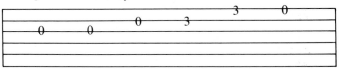

KEY OF D

A B C♯ D E F♯G A B C♯D E F♯G A

Clementine

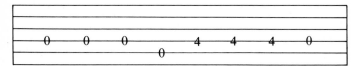

My Bonnie

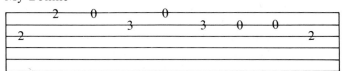

Red river valley

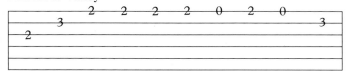

Banks of the Ohio

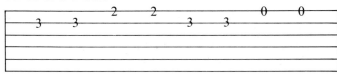

50

KEY OF A

A B C♯ D E F♯ G♯ A   A B C♯ D E F♯ G♯ A

Molly Malone

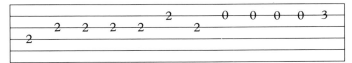

Michael, row the boat ashore

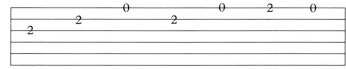

Kumbaya

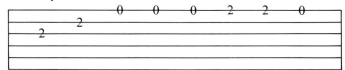

He's got the whole world in His hands

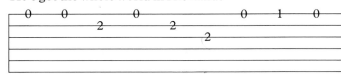

KEY OF E

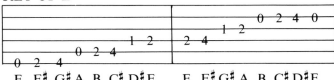
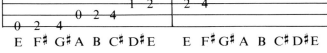

E F♯ G♯ A B C♯ D♯ E   E F♯ G♯ A B C♯ D♯ E

I used to play

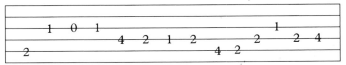

Amazing grace

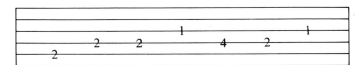

Midnight special

Scales

Although many music students try to avoid practising scales, this is still one of the best exercises for anyone learning to play a musical instrument.

Playing scales will help you get to know the notes on the guitar. It is good practice for your ear, teaches you speed and is the fastest and most effective way to improve technically.

The more you practise scales, the more fun it becomes. There is a certain satisfaction to be found in improving on the way you play your scales. It will definitely be worth your while to practise scales for a few minutes every time you pick up your guitar.

SCALE OF C

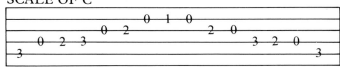

Each of the fingers on your left hand plays the notes behind one specific fret. When playing scales on the guitar, it is important for the left hand to stay in one position.

For variation you can play the basic scale in different ways.

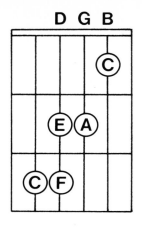

D G B

first finger

second finger

third finger

If you are particularly interested in fingerpicking or classical guitar, then the best way to play a scale is to alternate between your i and m fingers:

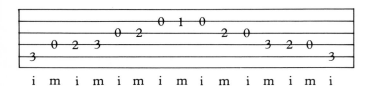

i m i m i m i m i m i m i m i m i

Or you can play the scale with a plectrum using downward strokes:

SCALE OF G

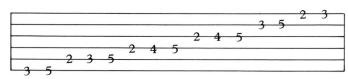

Or play downward and upward strokes alternately:

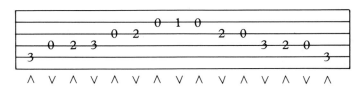

Or play according to a rhythmic pattern, with long notes on the downward strokes and short notes on the upward strokes. This is a very effective exercise for anyone who aims to become a lead guitarist.

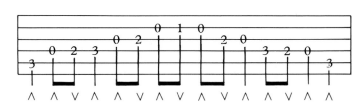

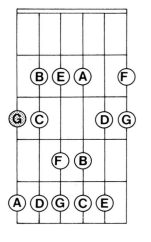

first finger

second finger

third finger

fourth finger

52

This scale pattern is similar to a bar chord in the sense that when you know it in one position, you only have to play the same pattern lower down or higher up on the fretboard to play the scale of a different key.

The first note on the bass string determines the position and key of the scale. The first note of the scale at the bottom of page 52 is G, so this is, therefore, the scale of G.

When you want to play the scale of D, for example, you only have to move the whole pattern up so that the first note of the scale is played behind the tenth fret.

Here are another two scale patterns that can be played in different positions:

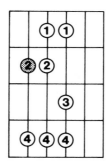
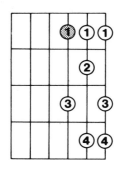

Connecting notes

A simple fingerpicking or strumming pattern can be effectively supplemented by playing connecting notes between the bass notes of the chords.

Practise the three examples given here. When you understand the principle you will then be able to add connecting notes, in appropriate places, when you are playing songs.

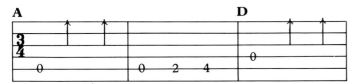

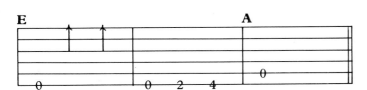

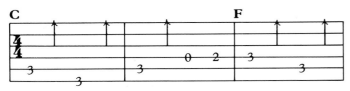

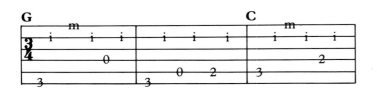

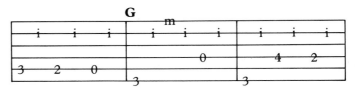

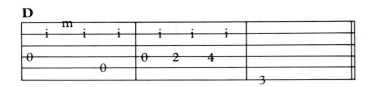

Melody techniques

REST STROKES AND FREE STROKES

A free stroke is the method of plucking a string where the finger continues to move past the next string.

Rest strokes are used by classical guitarists in particular to make the notes of a melody stand out. In a rest stroke, the finger that plucks the string comes to rest on the next string.

Completion: free stroke

Preparation: rest stroke and free stroke

Completion: rest stroke

SLUR

The slur is used in all kinds of guitar styles. After a note has been played, the left-hand finger is pulled off the string in such a way that the string sounds.

A slur is indicated by a curved line connecting the two notes:

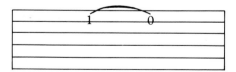

In the above example, the first note is played as normal. The left-hand finger is then pulled off the second string so that the open string sounds. In other words, the second note is not played by the right hand.

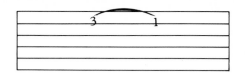

In this example, the first finger must already be in position when the first note is played. The third finger is then pulled off the string so that the C note sounds.

The slur is a handy technique with which classical guitarists can achieve a certain flow in a piece of music, and lead guitarists can gain more speed.

LIGADO

The ligado is the opposite of the slur. Instead of pulling the left-hand finger off the string, it is hammered down onto the string to make it sound.

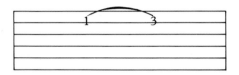

In the above example, the first note is played as normal and the third finger is then hammered down to form the next note.

SLIDE

The slide is a simple technique in which the first note is played and, while the string is still sounding, the left-hand finger is slid either up or down the fretboard to the next note.

VIBRATO

Vibrato is used to make a note sound for a longer time and to add feeling and expression to long melody notes. The left hand is moved rapidly to and fro horizontally, while the finger continues to press on the string.

STRING BENDING

This technique is very popular with lead guitarists. When the note has been played, the string is bent upwards – towards the thumb – so that the pitch of the string becomes a semitone or a whole tone higher. It is very important that the note to which you bend should be the right pitch. Perfect this by comparing the note you have played to the note on the next fret. String bending is usually done on the three treble strings, and the third finger is the one most often used to bend the string because it is the strongest. The first and second fingers can, however, also be placed on the string to assist the third finger.

Sight-reading made easier

NOTES

Start by getting to know the name of each line and space of the staff by heart. They are the basic "words" in the language of sheet music.

Take a clean sheet of paper and cover the page with staves of five lines each. Draw dots on the lines and in the spaces at random.

From memory, write the name of each note below the note. When you're finished, repeat the exercise on another piece of paper. Keep at it until you are sure you know each note by heart.

RHYTHM

Before you start sight-reading a piece of music, first go through it tapping the rhythm of the notes with your finger on a book or table. This way, you will familiarise yourself with the rhythm in advance, which helps a lot when you start to sight-read the piece.

Sight-reading

A piece of sheet music looks like Greek to a beginner. However, it is not that difficult to learn to sight-read. Once you have grasped the basic principles, it is really quite easy to follow written music. After that, it is merely a question of practice.

Being able to sight-read has quite a few advantages. Sheet music is the standard method of writing music – for *all* musical instruments. In fact, it is a good way to record your own musical ideas and compositions. The way in which music is written down will teach you a lot about music theory. And if you want to learn to play classical guitar, it is essential that you are able to sight-read.

The names of the notes

Sheet music is written on a staff which comprises five lines with four spaces between them. The sign at the beginning of the staff is the G clef, as opposed to the F or bass clef. The G clef is so named because the sign starts on the line for the G note.

Each of the lines and spaces represents a note:

Since there are fewer notes on the staff than on the guitar, *leger lines* are added at the top or bottom of the staff, where necessary.

The notes on the six open strings of the guitar are as follows (music for the guitar is written one octave higher than it sounds):

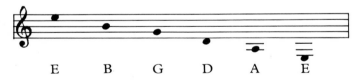

On the left of the staff, two further details are indicated: the key signature and the time signature.

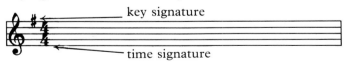

KEY SIGNATURE

The key signature indicates in which key the music should be played.

If there is no sharp (♯) or flat (♭) sign, then the music is in the key of C major or A minor.

If there is only one sharp, then the music is in the key of G major or E minor. The sharp sign will be on the line representing the F note. This means that all F notes in the piece of music must be played as F♯ .

The keys commonly found in guitar music are:

A note that must be played as a sharp or flat but that does not form part of the key signature will be indicated by a sharp or flat sign next to the note, and wherever that note occurs in the remainder of the measure, it should be played sharp or flat.

The sign ♮ means that a note that should be either sharp or flat according to the key signature, should *not* be played as a sharp or flat for the remainder of the measure.

TIME SIGNATURE

The time signature indicates the rhythm of the music. It is always written in the form of a fraction. Four over four means there are four crotchets (quarter notes) in each measure, in other words, quadruple time. Three over four means there are three crotchets to the bar, in other words, triple time. Six over eight means there are six quavers (eight notes) to the bar, which is six-eight time. Quadruple time is sometimes indicated by a capital C, standing for "common time".

The length, or value, of each note is indicated by the way the note is drawn. The signs are:

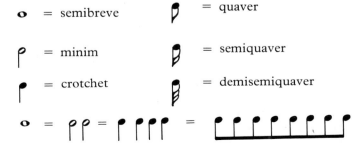

A crotchet lasts for one beat. A semibreve will, therefore, last for four beats, a minim for two beats and a quaver for half a beat, which is counted as an "and".

1 2 3 4   1 2 3 4 +   1 2 + 3 4

Measures, or *bars*, are indicated by vertical lines. The total duration of all the notes in a bar is always the amount indicated by the time signature.

Notes with dots after them are called *dotted notes*. Such a note lasts its own value plus half of it. The value of a dotted minim is, therefore, one minim plus a crotchet.

A note that lasts longer than a bar is connected to the note in the next bar by means of a *tie*. The first note lasts for the value of both notes. The second note is, therefore, not played, but should sound for the total duration of both notes.

EXAMPLES FOR PRACTICE

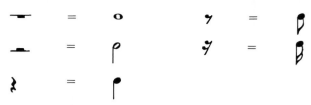

OTHER SIGNS

This sign means that the preceding section should be repeated.

A small number above a note indicates which left-hand finger should depress the note.

A small line in front of a note means that the finger used to depress the previous note, should slide up or down on the same string in order to hold down the next note.

Amazing grace   *Traditional*

Jingle bells   *Traditional*

56

Ode to joy

Beethoven

Silent night, Holy night

F. Gruber

Jesu, joy of man's desiring

J. S. Bach

6 INSTRUMEN-TAL PIECES

Instrumental pieces add a whole new dimension to a guitarist's performance. So it is a really good idea to include a few pieces in your repertoire where the guitar does all the talking and you don't have to sing along at all.

In a solo instrumental piece for the guitar, the right hand plays both the melody *and* the rhythm, in contrast with the piano where the left hand plays the rhythm and chords, and the right hand plays the melody.

In classical guitar music, the melody and notes of the chords form an integrated whole. Each note is important.

In adaptations of songs for solo performance, on the other hand, the notes of the melody should stand out clearly from the bass and filler notes. The notes of the melody should be accentuated because it is the tunefulness of the piece that gives it its distinct character. The thumb should play a strong and steady beat on the bass strings.

The pieces included in this chapter appear in order of intricacy. Don't be in too much of a hurry to learn *all* the pieces. Choose one piece at a time and practise it until you can play it fluently and with ease.

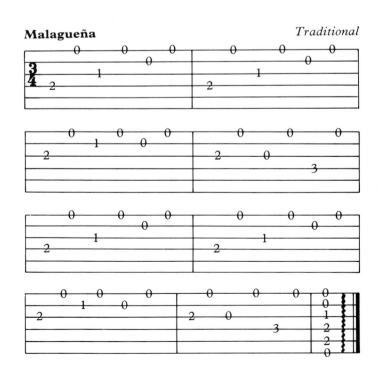

Malagueña   *Traditional*

On top of old Smokey   *Traditional*

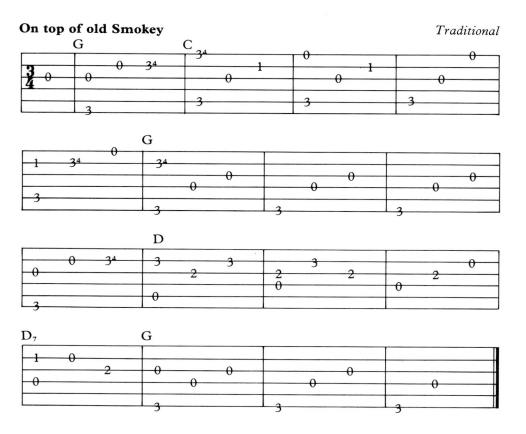

House of the Rising Sun   *Traditional*

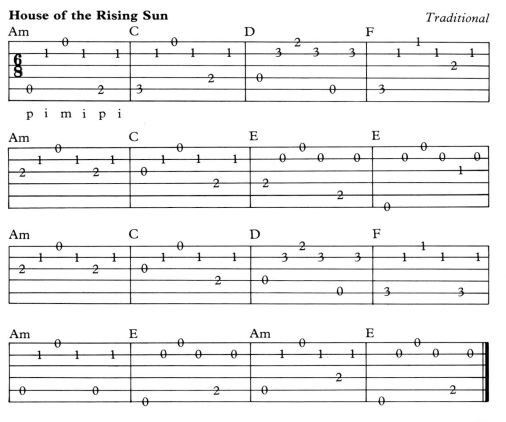

When the saints go marching in   *Traditional*

A

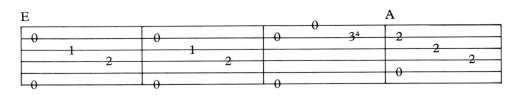

E   A

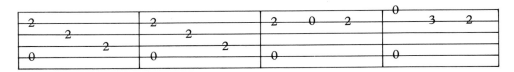

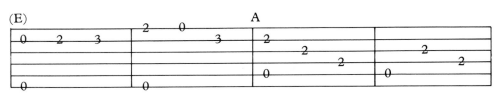

(E)   A

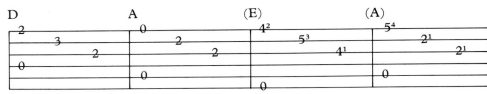

D   A   (E)   (A)

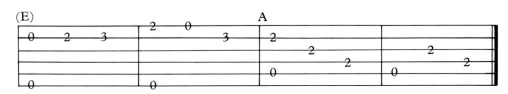

(E)   A   A

60

Minuet in G   *J. S. Bach*

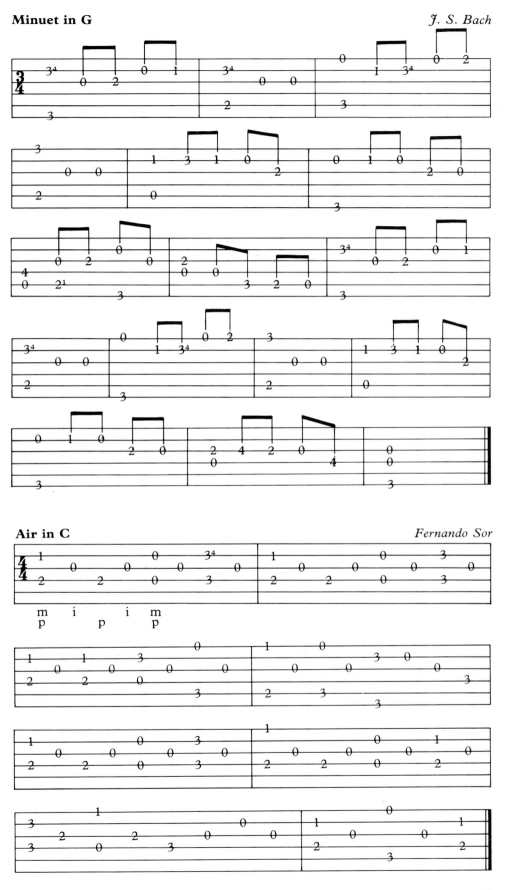

Air in C   *Fernando Sor*

Ecossaise   *Guiliani*

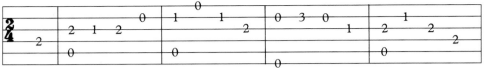

Fine

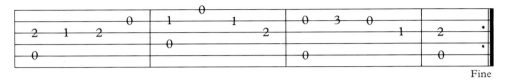

D.C. al Fine

Arietta   *Kuffner*

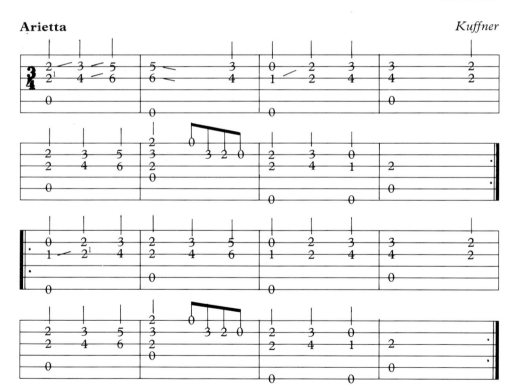

62

Greensleeves

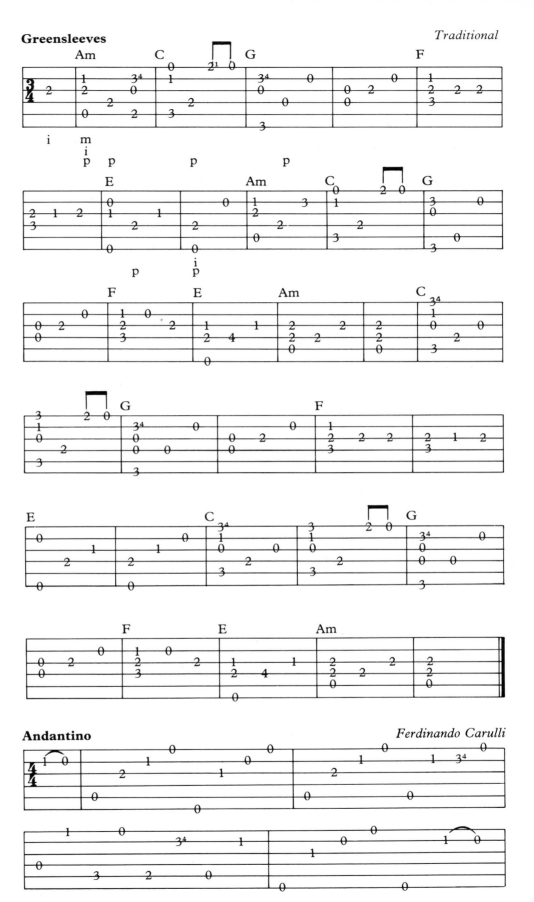

Andantino

Ferdinando Carulli

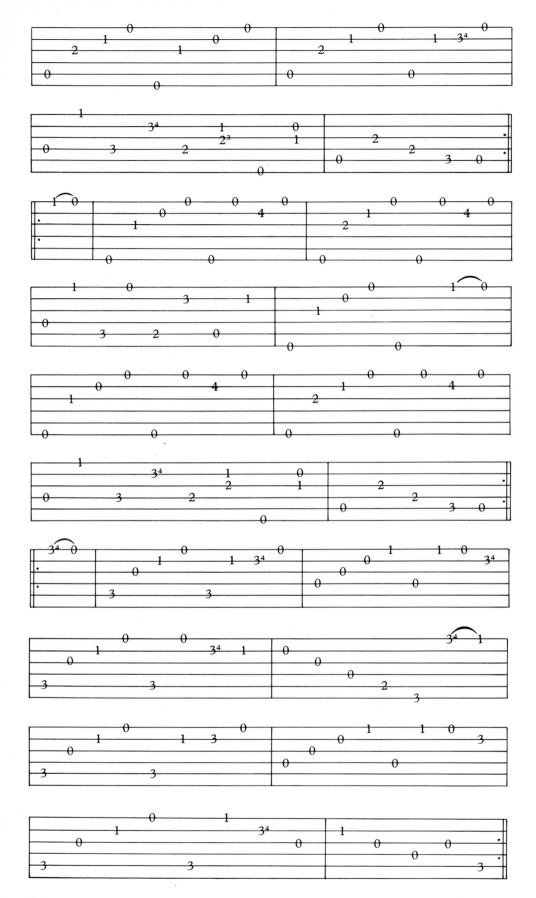

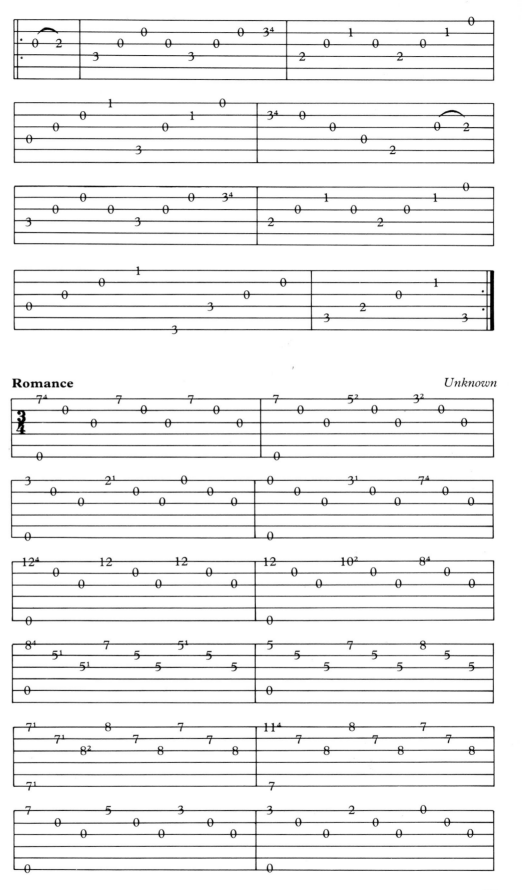

Romance *Unknown*

7 SONGS

One of the best ways to keep up your enthusiasm for your guitar playing is to learn new songs continually. This will also increase your repertoire and broaden your musical frame of reference.

It is important to have a recording of the song you want to learn to play. Some songs are so simple (take the traditional songs in chapter three, for example) that you can learn to play them from memory. However, you will generally find it much easier to learn to play and sing a song if you have listened to it carefully a few times first. By doing this, you will also learn a lot about interpretation, tempo and phrasing, and will often come across interesting new techniques.

Concentrate, therefore, on music you have on record or tape, or that you can get hold of by some other means. It is a good idea to collect a number of songs by one of your favourite artistes. You could try to get hold of a book featuring the songs of this artiste. If your local music shop does not have the book in stock, they could order it for you. Also look around in music shops for sheet music books with the kind of songs you would like to play.

Most of the songs in this chapter have been recorded by well-known artistes, in most cases, by the person who composed the song. *House of the Rising Sun* was a big hit for The Animals and later for Frigid Pink; Bob Dylan also recorded it on his very first LP. *Sailing* was a big success in the seventies for Rod Stewart. *Scarborough Fair* was a hit for Simon and Garfunkel, Cat Stevens did well with *Morning has broken* and Donovan made the best-known recording of *Donna donna*. *Greensleeves* and *Jamaica farewell* have been recorded by a number of artistes. If you can't get hold of a recording of these songs, try to find someone who knows them well enough to be able to teach them to you.

Other guitarists are, of course, one of the best sources of new songs. Even if you do not know any other guitarists yet, you are bound to meet some sooner or later. Don't let chances like that slip through your fingers – learn as much as you can from every guitarist you meet. Most guitarists will be only too pleased to teach you the songs they most enjoy playing. If there is not too much difference between your skills and theirs, you might even be able to start playing together. And then you will discover that making music together is more than enough compensation for all the hours of struggling and frustration.

Morning has broken
Traditional/Eleanor Farjeon

Intro: C F G E Am G₇ C F C

  C   Am Dm G   F C
Morning has broken, like the first morning,

         Em Am Dsus   D G
Blackbird has spoken like the first bird.

  C   F   C   Am D
Praise for the singing, praise for the morning,

  G   C F G₇   C
Praise for them springing fresh from the world.

Sweet the rain's new fall, sunlit from heaven,
Like the first dewfall on the first grass.
Praise for the sweetness of the wet garden,
Sprung in completeness where His feet pass.

Mine is the sunlight, mine is the morning,
Born of the one light Eden saw play.
Praise with elation, praise every morning,
God's re-creation of the new day.

C

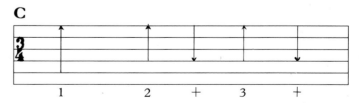

      1   2   +   3   +

Jamaica farewell
Traditional

     C   F
Down the way where the nights are gay

        G   C
And the sun shines daily on the mountain top,

            F
I took a trip on a sailing ship,

        G   C
And when I reached Jamaica I made a stop.

               Dm
But I'm sad to say I'm on my way,

   G₇   C
I won't be back for many a day.

                Dm
My heart is down, my head is turning around,

       G₇   C
I had to leave a little girl in Kingston Town.

Down by the market you can hear
Ladies cry out while on their heads they bear
Akki rice, salt fish are nice
And the rum is fine any time of year.

Sounds of laughter everywhere,
As the dancing girls swing to and fro.
I must declare my heart is there,
Though I've been from Main to Mexico.

C

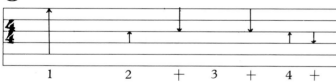

Donna donna
Traditional

Am   E   Am   E
On a wagon bound for market

   Am   Dm   Am E Am
There's a calf with a mournful eye;

               E   Am   E
High above him there's a swallow

   Am   Dm Am   E Am
Winging swiftly through the sky.

  G   Am
   How the winds are laughing

    G   Am
   They laugh with all their might;

  G   Am
   Love and laugh the whole day through

             E   Am
   And half the summer's night

   E   Am
Donna, donna, donna, donna,

   Dm   Am
Donna, donna, donna, do.

   E   Am
Donna, donna, donna, donna,

   Dm   E   Am E Am E
Donna, donna, donna, do.

Stop complaining, said the farmer,
Who told you a calf to be?
Why don't you have wings to fly with,
Like the swallow so proud and free?

Calves are easily bound and slaughtered,
Never knowing the reason why;
But whoever treasures freedom,
Like the swallow has learnt to fly.

Am   **E**

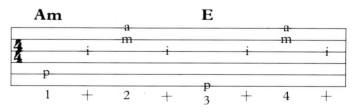

Me and Bobby McGee
Kris Kristofferson/Fred Foster

A
Busted flat in Baton Rouge, heading for the trains,

                                E
Feeling nearly as faded as my jeans.

Bobby thumbed a diesel down, just before it rained,

                        A
Took us all the way to New Orleans.

I took my harpoon out of my dirty red bandanna

                    A₇   D
And was blowing sad while Bobby sang the blues;

                                      A
With them wind-shield wipers slapping time and Bobby

clapping hands

        E   A
We finally sang up every song that driver knew.

   D   A
Freedom's just another word for nothing left to lose;

   E   A
Nothing ain't worth nothing but it's free.

   D   A
Feeling good was easy, Lord, when Bobby sang the

   blues;

   E
Feeling good was good enough for me,

                              A
Good enough for me and my Bobby McGee.

From the coalmines of Kentucky to the California sun,
Bobby shared the secrets of my soul;
Standing right beside me through everything I done,
And every night she kept me from the cold.
Then somewhere near Salinas, Lord, I let her slip away,
Looking for the home I hope she'll find,
And I'd trade all my tomorrows for a single yesterday,
Holding Bobby's body close to mine.

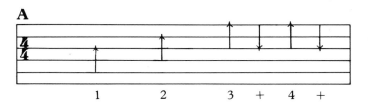

Scarborough Fair
Traditional

Dm   C   Dm
Are you going to Scarborough Fair,

                   G   Dm
Parsley, sage, rosemary and thyme;

           F   C
Remember me to the one who lives there,

Dm   C   Dm
She once was a true love of mine.

Tell her to make me a cambric shirt,
Parsley, sage, rosemary and thyme;
Without no seam or fine needlework,
Then she'll be a true love of mine.

Tell her to find me an acre of land,
Parsley, sage, rosemary and thyme;
Between the salt water and the sea strand,
Then she'll be a true love of mine.

Tell her to plow it with a lamb's horn,
Parsley, sage, rosemary and thyme;
And sow it all over with peppercorn,
Then she'll be a true love of mine.

Tell her to reap it with a sickle of leather,
Parsley, sage, rosemary and thyme;
And gather it all in a bunch of heather,
Then she'll be a true love of mine.

Dm

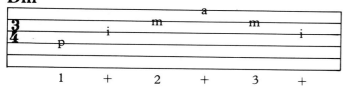

Mull of Kintyre
McCartney/Laine

         A
Mull of Kintyre,

          D   A
Oh mist rolling in from the sea;

                D
My desire is always to be here,

        A
Oh Mull of Kintyre.

 A
Far have I travelled and much have I seen,

 D   A
Dark, distant mountains with valleys of green;

Vast painted deserts the sun sets on fire,

         D   E   A
As he carries me home to the Mull of Kintyre.

Sweep through the heather like deer in the glen;
Carry me back to the days I knew then.
Nights when we sang like a heavenly choir
Of the life and the times of the Mull of Kintyre.

Smiles in the sunshine and tears in the rain;
Still take me back where my memories remain.
Flickering embers grow higher and higher
As they carry me back to the Mull of Kintyre.

A

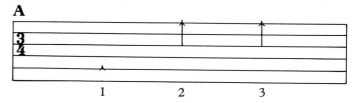

Sailing
G. Sutherland

```
        C            Am
I am sailing, I am sailing,

          F              C
Home again, 'cross the sea.

       D              Am
I am sailing, stormy waters,

         Dm           C  G
To be near you, to be free.
```

I am flying, I am flying,
Like a bird, 'cross the sky,
I am flying, passing high clouds,
To be with you, to be free.

Can you hear me, can you hear me?
Through the dark night, far away.
I am dying, forever trying,
To be with you, who can say?

C

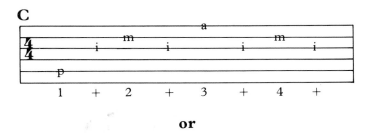

or

C

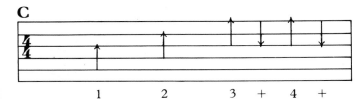

House of the Rising Sun
Traditional

```
      Am  C       D    F
There is a house in New Orleans

      Am     C     E
They call the Rising Sun.

      Am    C       D       F
It's been the ruin of many a poor girl,

        Am  E       Am E
And God knows I'm one.
```

My mother she's a tailor,
She sews my new blue jeans.
My father he's a gambling man,
Way down in New Orleans.

The only thing a gambler needs,
Is to go from town to town.
And the only time he's satisfied,
Is when he drinks his liquor down.

Go tell my baby sister
Not to do what I have done.
Shun that house in New Orleans
They call the Rising Sun.

I've got one foot on the platform,
The other foot on the train.
I'm going back to New Orleans,
To wear that ball and chain.

Am

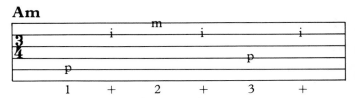

Greensleeves
Traditional

Dm   F   C   Am
Alas, my love, you do me wrong

       Dm   A₇
To cast me off so discourteously,

       Dm   F   C   Am
When I have courted you so long,

    Dm   A₇   Dm
Delighted in your company.

      F   C   Am
Greensleeves was all my joy,

      Dm   A₇
Greensleeves was my delight.

      F   C   Am
Greensleeves was my heart of gold,

       Dm   A₇   Dm
And who but my lady Greensleeves.

I have been ready at your hand,
To grant whatever you would crave;
I have both wagered life and land,
Your love and goodwill for to have.

Well, I will pray to God on high
That you my constancy mayst see;
And that yet once before I die,
You will vouchsafe to love me.

So Greensleeves farewell, adieu,
May good fortune prosper thee,
For I am still thy lover true,
Oh, come once again and love me.

Dm

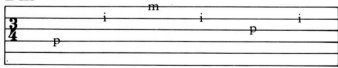